GARY JAY POOL

THE 3rd HERD

Explosive Ordnance Disposal

Ramblings of my everyday life

while serving with an EOD unit in
Viet Nam

By GARY JAY POOL

THE 3RD HERD

Explosive Ordnance Disposal

Published by Pool Publishing, Tabor, Iowa 51653
Printed in the United States of America

Library of Congress cataloguing in publication data

ISBN: 978-1-7321574-2-2

THE MEANING OF THE
E O D UNIT BADGE

The Wreath
Symbolic of the achievements and laurels gained in minimizing accident potentials, through the ingenuity and devotion to duty of its members. It is in memory of those EOD officer and military personnel who gave their lives while performing EOD duties.

The Bomb
Copied from the design of the World War II Bomb Disposal Badge, the bomb represents the historic and major objective of the EOD attack, the unexploded bomb. The three fins represent the major areas of nuclear, conventional, and chemical/biological interests.

Lightning Bolts
Symbolize the potential destructive power of the bomb and the courage and professionalism of EOD personnel in their endeavors to reduce hazards as well as render explosive ordnance harmless.

The Shield
Represents the EOD mission, to prevent a detonation and protect the surrounding area and property to the utmost.

Walter Gee, Mike Nichols, Gary Pool,
Dave Tipton, John Claffy and Dick Hause
The Boys of '69-'70 3rd Ord

2009 National EOD Association
Reunion

Branson, Missouri

DEDICATION

These writings are the result of my association with EOD men everywhere, but in particular it is the 3rd Ord EOD and the men who served in Viet Nam who made these stories possible. It was these men in the bad as well as the good times that forged an everlasting bond of brotherhood. It is my hope that anyone who reads these simple tales will gain some degree of understanding of the connection that is shared by this tiny group of men.

I would like to thank all of the 3rd Ord EOD men for their patience and understanding that gave direction to my life in these post Viet Nam years.

ACKNOWLEDGMENTS

I would like to extend a special thank you to my wife Jan and daughters Pam, Lorna, Loretta and Andi, for all their help in putting this book together including artwork, web design, editing and marketing. Without them I would be lost. Their opinions, support and encouragement helps make my books possible.

Terminology

APC: Armored Personnel Carrier
ARVN: Army the Republic of Viet Nam
CO: Commanding Officer
DMZ: Demilitarized Zone
EM: CLUB: Enlisted Men's Club
EOD: Explosive Ordnance Disposal
HOOCH: Sleeping quarters
HUEY: Specific type of helicopter
LZ: Landing Zone
MOS: Military Occupational Specialty
MP: Military Police
MPC: Military Pay Script
MSGT: Master Sergeant
NCO: Non-commissioned Officer
OD: Olive Drab
PDO: Property Disposal Office
PFC: Private First Class
PX: Post Exchange
RSP: Render Safe Procedure
SFC: Sergeant First Class
SGT: Sergeant
SOP: Standard Operating Procedure
SSGT: Staff Sergeant
TDY: Temporary Duty
VC: Viet Cong
VIP: Very Important Personnel
WP: White Phosphorus

Ten years ago I wrote Xuc May, a book about my experiences serving in an Explosive Ordnance Disposal Unit (bomb disposal) during the Viet Nam War. The book was published and sold as a fundraiser for injured bomb disposal personnel returning from the Middle East. Xuc May sold well and we were able to make a substantial donation to the families of recuperating EOD vets no matter the branch of service.

It was a rewarding experience, not only being able to tour one of their rehabilitation training facilities in San Antonio, but meeting hundreds of Viet Nam veterans while doing book talks and book signings. It became clear from the feedback at these events that the readers wanted more stories with more information.

The original edition of Xuc May went out of print a few years ago, so we could no longer honor the ongoing requests for a copy. I have allowed a decade to pass while working on other writing projects which prevented further work on two of my favorite subjects, EOD and the Viet Nam War.

Life moves on, people pass, and opinions change, so we have decided to re-release the original Xuc May, while at the same time publish The 3rd Herd, Explosive Ordnance Disposal, another book of stories and updates in hopes of satisfying those people interested in E.O.D and the Viet Nam War.

To be perfectly honest the original Xuc May was, as I said, a fundraiser. That association has cordially ended and we wish to make it clear that the profits from the re-released Xuc May and the new book will be the sole property of Pool's Publishing to be spent or donated as we see fit.

During our exposure with the public while promoting Xuc May we were delighted to hear of the female interest in these stories, but also realized that many of the stories were not fully explained, thinking our readers would be mostly those with some military connections. This was a grievous error and I do apologize for this failure. With that said, I will attempt to give better information in The 3rd Herd.

In addition, as a lead-in to The 3rd Herd, I have found it necessary to include some of the stories from the original book that will offer a clearer picture of the events.

THE 3rd HERD

Explosive Ordnance Disposal

South Viet Nam

GARY JAY POOL

Contents

HISTORY OF EXPLOSIVES...................... 15

BUT WHO AM I 21

FORT BLISS 25

AFTER BASIC... 31

MY HOME IN-COUNTRY 41

ASSIGNED TO THE 3RD ORD................ 47

DESTINED TO BE IN THE 3RD ORD...... 53

FRAGGINGS... 57

COMPANY CLERK.................................... 63

MORTAR FLARE PROJECTILE 67

NEVER SAFE FROM HARM..................... 69

DEADLY DET CORD 71

PACKAGE FROM HOME......................... 77

GRAVES REGISTRATION STANDOFF..... 83

CHINOOK RIDE....................................... 91

SKY CRANE HEIST.................................. 95

FRIENDLY FIRE 99

BOB HOPE USO SHOW......................... 105

ROAD CLOSED 119

MILITARY ISSUE.................................... 123

THAI FOOD 133

IT'S MY HAMBURGER........................... 137

THE BOLDEST EOD MAN 143

CHEMICAL WARFARE 155

GARBAGE CANS...................................163

SELF PROPELLED 155 169

A WILD GOOSE CHASE.......................171

DEADLY PILE 181

MALARIA PILL 187

FIELD EXPEDIENCE 191

ASSASSINATION TEAM 199

MEETING THE AUSSIE'S......................207

WHITE MICE 215

SAFING A GRENADE 219

DEEP SORROW 227

BOMBLETS 229

SURGERY ON THE SIDEWALK..............237

OUT OF SHAPE 245

MACV BUILDING 253

SMITTY TAKES A DIP 257

EQUIPMENT 263

SHOTGUN SHELLS...............................269

BRIDGES...275

DON'T GET OUT OF THE JEEP BOYS ..279

AMMUNITION DEPOT..........................285

ARMED AND READY 291

NCO CLUB..295

HARVESTING BOWLS 299

MP's 303

L.B.J. 305

TEACHING 311

VIET NAM EOD VETERANS REUNION . 313

TRIBUTE TO MASTER JACK 317

TRIBUTE TO ART MACKSEY 321

TRIBUTE TO DICK KORNMANN 325

TRIBUTE TO SMITTY 329

TRIBUTE TO JOHN CLAFFY 333

TRIBUTE TO JIM POINDEXTER 337

A SPECIAL THANK YOU 339

AN EOD MAN 341

HISTORY OF EXPLOSIVES

You might call this an introduction to Explosive Ordnance Disposal, or possibly a familiarization with bomb disposal. As with all things the human mind explores, there are differences of opinion on every subject. The statements I make in this writing may not be totally correct but are the facts as I believe them to be.

Most military historians give the Chinese credit for the discovery of black powder in the ninth century and is often considered the most dangerous explosive to work with. That seems like an outlandish statement when you consider all the thousands of chemical compounds that have been developed over the years. Black Powder or gun powder, as it is often called, is not a high explosive; instead it is a low explosive that needs a container or some type of confinement to produce a detonation.

High explosives, which includes most of those developed after black powder can detonate without confinement but they normally are less sensitive and require an initiator or shock to produce a rapid chemical decompensation of their chemical ingredients.

Now I realize this is a little deep in the subject of explosives and is done to make the average reader comprehend the basic handling of explosives. Suffice it to say, when dealing with any type of explosive, anything can and will go wrong, no matter how careful a person might be. Explosive Ordnance is manufactured with the intent to kill or destroy and should be relegated to those who are willing to be killed or destroyed.

Bomb disposal dates back to at least the Civil War when soldiers volunteered to disarm land and water mines. Organized disposal became more prevalent in the Second World War when the United States began to train personnel to deactivate ordnance. At the same time the British government organized their bomb disposal in response to all the German bombs and missiles that failed to function on impact and became buried in the soil or under piles of debris, hence becoming deadly unseen hazards to civilian and military movement. Those same German unexploded ordnance devices are still being unearthed better than seventy years after being dropped on Great Britain.

America, being blessed with two oceans between us and our enemies, had more time to prepare for an onslaught of hazardous ordnance, we had time to train a bomb disposal unit or at least that is what the American citizens were told. At that very moment the Japanese were releasing large balloons with crude timing mechanisms from ships in the Pacific Ocean which would drift on the prevailing westerly air streams and would release explosive and incendiary devices along the west coast of the United States. These weapons started fires in some of the western states. One balloon managed to reach as far inland as Omaha, Nebraska. All of this was strictly secret, even to the degree that the press kept it under their hat.

The British however were not so fortunate with only the English Channel separating the two belligerent countries; a lot of dud ordnance fell within their country. Many civilians were injured and killed by these devices, so much so that it was impossible to keep news stories out of the press. It was clear that the British government had to respond immediately and they did so by forming up a group of ordnance officers who knew explosives and fuses. Finding this group too small for the task, the government called for civilian volunteers to attempt to rendering safe these potentially dangerous bombs. The volunteer units were mainly made up of men who were physically disabled or rejected from military duty.

It was a great idea except the British ordnance men knew very little about the operation of the German fuses and Hitler was not about to share the knowledge. So the disarming of fuses became a matter of trial and error. Sadly the errors cost many of the volunteers their lives.

When the Brits found an unexploded piece of German ordnance they would gently probe the area with long steel rods in order to determine the devices general location and depth. Metal detectors, as well as other electronic instruments were still in their infancy and ground penetrating radar, so commonly in use today, was unheard of.

Once the bomb was located the team would start to excavate the area by hand. They dug a square shaft straight down while reinforcing the sides with planks and timbers until reaching the bomb. The shaft might be only a couple of feet deep or possibly ten to twenty feet under the surface depending on the type of soil, the angle of penetration and the weight of the device.

The Navy EOD School had special classes which taught us to dig and support such excavations plus the correct terminology for a rope, a line, or a hawser and Lord knows how many other items the U.S. Navy has a unique title for. This course was called rigging and digging, one of the few areas where I excelled due to my intimate knowledge of such tools.

However, once the shaft was dug and reinforced some poor soul would descend into the hole with a tool kit, a light, and possibly a telephone wire that allowed him to give step by step specifics of his attempt to render safe this device to someone outside the shaft who was listening from a safe distance. These poor souls were left alone at the bottom of a dark dirty shaft to experiment on a highly engineered and precision manufactured piece of German ordnance. They would turn a specific screw one turn then report that all went well, another turn and another report until the screw was removed or there was a large ground shaking subterranean explosion accompanied by a geyser of dirt.

I have seen films of these brave British volunteers and have often wondered if they were, say ten feet in the ground surrounded by vertical dirt walls when a 2500 kg bomb detonated, was any attempt made to retrieve the body or did the authorities merely fill the shaft with dirt and move on to the next experiment. I don't mean to make light of these incidents for I have the greatest respect for those who, out of love of country and the desire to serve the war effort in any way possible, gave their lives in a questionable program.

Plaque located in downtown Dundee, Nebraska indicating a Japanese balloon bomb exploded there in 1945 over 50th & Underwood Streets. (a suburb of Omaha, Nebraska)

BUT WHO AM I

But who am I, you might ask. I am Gary Jay Pool, the author of Xuc May, and an Iowa native. My father was a poor hired farmhand and World War Two veteran who believed a person's only right was long hours of back-breaking labor. My mother was a frustrated house wife who realized she had musical and literary talents that she set aside in order to make a proper home for her family.

We moved several times in the early years of my youth because father had an itchy foot while mother, on the other hand, resisted making a ten mile drive to town once a week to do the shopping. She loved music but father was tone death and said every tune was just noise to be tolerated. But they loved each other, celebrating over fifty years of marriage, finding enjoyment in the simplest moments of life. They stressed the need for education to my sister and me, always insisting we do the right thing in all instances.

After high school and a year of work, I enrolled in a junior college for a couple of years.

But I quickly became disenchanted with all the anti-war talk, not only from the students but also from the instructors. When I could no longer accept their theories and the growing anti-American propaganda, I felt it was time to leave the halls of higher education to those of little experience with all the answers. It was time to go out in the world to seek the truth.

The harsh truth, I discovered, was an unwritten rule that unless you had been in the military, or had a draft deferment, no one would hire a draft-age young man. My parents could not afford to support me and finding even odd jobs in the winter proved impossible. It was now time to buck the tide of friends and neighbors who called me a fool and an idiot for joining the military rather than going to the National Guards or waiting to be drafted. It was, I thought, the proper thing to do in light of the fact the war was all the talk, and all the newspaper and television coverage was being provided by people who knew little to nothing about Viet Nam. They had never been there and were unable to find the small country on a globe the week before. No, it was time for discovering the truth about the Viet Nam War. Besides, at twenty one years of age we all felt indestructible so I enlisted in the United States Army.

6 March 1967 a small group of newly inducted soldiers were loaded onto an antique train car for our trip to basic training. We left

Omaha, Nebraska heading south and within a few minutes passed through my home town of Bartlett, Iowa - population less the one hundred souls. It was the first of many unique experiences the Army provided, and one I'll never forget as I watched the little hamlet flash by the railcar windows. Time elapsed - no more than five seconds.

We changed trains in Kansas City then began moving west across Kansas and Nebraska on our way to Casper Wyoming. At this stop we were hustled onto a Pullman sleeper car for an overnight run south into New Mexico. The train cars were ancient and the food non-existent until we arrived at Albuquerque where the Army had graciously arranged for us to eat in the railroad depot dining room. We were served wilted lettuce salad with lady bug dressing and a slab of warm mutton that tasted for all the world like a boiled wool sweater. Protests were duly ignored except to load the whole group back on the train.

This train moved slowly across the New Mexico desert finally arriving at El Paso, Texas after dark where we were loaded into large busses to be deposited at the main base of Ft. Bliss, Texas.

This was my initiation to the world of graft and crooked contractors that became the norm rather than the exception during the Viet Nam War years. We were transported miles out of our way, given substandard vehicles and no food or drinks unless you bribed one of the train crew to supply beer at triple the going price.

At Ft. Bliss we were hustled into a large gym with a couple hundred other inductees where a Mexican Sergeant who no one could hear or understand in the wee hours of the morning gave instructions of what to expect during our time at Ft. Bliss. Somewhere in this Sergeant's introduction he held aloft a large white pill before telling us to form up at the water fountains.

At the drinking fountains each man was watched by an NCO to be certain that everyone did indeed take this unknown pill. This took a great deal of time as each man swallowed the prescribed pill to the great pleasure of the inspecting noncom. It was only later that we learned the PILL was an experimental drug and that the mumbling Mexican Sergeant had explained that we were part of a test and that we had agreed to participate in this grand experiment.

FORT BLISS

By taking this unknown pill, we had our first taste of the Army's idea of volunteering. I never knew, but was told later the pill was to help prevent spinal meningitis which Ft. Bliss had been battling for some time. To counter the outbreak, trainees were also made to stand two feet apart whenever in formation and although we had bunk beds, we could only occupy alternating bunks. The bottom bunk on the first set of bunk beds was assigned a man but no one could sleep on the top bunk. The second set of bunk beds had a man assigned to the top bunk with no one occupying the bottom and so it went.

There were also sections of this huge base that had been quarantined. I and several others were lucky enough to be given special duty to enter these areas of quarantine to appropriate material that was needed elsewhere on base.

I became ill on my way home from basic training and being close to Offutt Air Force Base, I sought medical attention at their hospital. I was tested then told I had contracted spinal meningitis and would be held in the hospital under quarantine. That was until they discovered that I was in the Army and not the Air Force, at which point the powers that be gave me a shot and sent me home. It seems the Air Force didn't have jurisdiction over me or more likely didn't want to get involved. But in any case, I was feeling better by the next day and all was forgotten; must have been one powerful shot of penicillin.

The first few days of basic training at Fort Bliss was like every movie story that one hears of indoctrination. Standing in long lines to be issued ill-fitting uniforms and having your hair cut by graduates of the Western America Sheep Shearing School, because I'm sure there wasn't a barber in the bunch. Then more long lines for vaccinations, eye tests, and dental exams while listening to the tales of woe from half the company as to why they should never have been drafted in the first place and every one of these soldiers had a letter from their doctor back home to support their stated illness.

This was a learning experience, mostly learning who you could trust and who you couldn't, which men were outright liars and which individuals were dumb enough to believe every tall tale about the military and were foolish enough to repeat these fairy tales. I quickly learned the often stated line that the Army "can't do something" or that "the Army has to do something" was the biggest fallacy of all. In reality, at this point in time the U.S. Army could do whatever it wanted and often times would go against the stated belief just to prove how wrong these barracks lawyers were.

The big war build up was on and the Army had its hands full trying to train and care for this overload of new soldiers. Our mess hall was ranked as the worst in the battalion, our meals were bad and meager. The NCO's timed us in the mess hall. Time's up and you were ordered out, finished or not. Trying to eat bad food while being timed is bad enough but if you dumped food in the metal trash can as you scraped your plate on the way out of the mess hall, one of the ever-present cook's would yell and scream about wasting food. Some people are never happy. We were also punished for buying food from the PX or any other government approved on-base food outlet.

Ft. Bliss, located at El Paso, Texas is one of our largest military installations. Said to be larger than the state of Rhode Island, it covered a lot of land. I was located at Logan Heights, which was built on the sandy hillside of a barren mountain.

It was better than thirty miles to our rifle range and bivouac areas. The main headquarters, whose buildings were of picturesque Spanish two story construction with high vaulting arched walkways and red tile roofs were miles from the lack-luster barracks where we were eventually assigned. These fine structures were seldom visited by the average soldier except for the first day of basic and the last day, graduation. Of course, photographs of these inviting buildings were featured prominently in the hard bound annual, which every trooper was encouraged to buy.

I was fortunate enough to draw extra duty while in basic training, one tour was on Kitchen Police in our sub-standard mess hall, including the whole cadre of evil-tempered cooks. The second tour was, as we were told repeatedly, the "honor" of walking guard duty all night after a day of hard physical training. The men on guard duty were turned out for inspection and issued M-14 rifles with no ammunition.

Dress of the day was fatigues, helmets and web gear. After standing inspection we were loaded into a covered truck to be delivered to our assigned guard post. I drew the base toy land, which sounds easy enough, but turned out to be one of the hardest duties to walk. You were required to walk around the building for two hours or until you were relieved. Your enemy - a hand full of high ranking officers bratty kids who gathered to raise holy hell while doing their best to entice the guards into committing a tactical error such as reprimanding one of them, who would immediately report you to their parents.

We were warned ahead of time not to make any contact with these youths, no matter what they did to the toy land building or to you personally. As I have said, the new recruits knew very little about the rules and regulation of the Army but these young hoodlums could recite the book forward and backwards as they did their best to entrap the person on duty.

When finally relieved of guard post and loaded into the truck it would seem time to relax but you had to ride around the base to exchange the other guards before returning to your battalion area. Once in our own area, we were allowed ten minutes before it was time to load up in the truck to repeat the whole process. Ft. Bliss was so large it took all our down time to reset the guard for another tour. This continued all night with no sleep, then in the morning you stood another inspection before hurrying to the armors to turn in your weapon. At that time you rejoined your platoon for another days training, no dinner, no breakfast and no sleep before another day of relentless physical exercise but as I was often reminded, I did enlist, or more to the point, "you asked for it."

I was at Ft. Bliss up on Logan Heights for my basic training base. I would like to say basic at Bliss was the highlight of my enlistment, but it really wasn't. I admit to liking the El Paso area except I never really got over the feeling that this place was the bottom of some long-ago dried up ocean. It seemed the sand got into everything, including the food. I remember vividly eating watery Jell-O that crunched if you chewed it.

AFTER BASIC

I will try only for the sake of history to give the highlights of my service path before finally being assigned to the 3rd Herd.

The Army had generously offered to train me in some useful skill so I chose small arms repair. However when I enlisted, they neglected to tell me the school had been closed for over a year. Somehow orders for small arms repair was replaced with Ammunition Storage School to be attended after basic training.

I was fortunate to be given some leave time after basic training and before reporting to Redstone Arsenal for Ammunition Storage School in Huntsville, Alabama. Those few days of freedom allowed for a great deal of reflection on what I wanted from the Army. It was then I decided that if I must be in the Army, I wanted to be part of the war. I could never be satisfied expending three years of my life without experiencing the war, which was the reason of my military commitment. After leave I departed for Alabama with the intention of learning all I could about ammunition storage.

Red Stone Arsenal was a large base that spread out over thousands of acres of the beautiful Alabama countryside. It was also known as Rocket City, the home of Werner Von Braun, the head of our fledgling space program. I was lucky enough to work a detail that went to this newly built modern city, where they static test fired new experimental rocket engines that shook the ground for miles around during the firings.

I was assigned to a company school which is where a soldier is billeted while attending class in one of the many training facilities. Soldier students spent most of their time at their school, while only nights and weekends passed in the company area.

I thought Ammunition Storage School simple but interesting as they taught the basics of ammunition and explosives. This was a very rudiment instruction to be sure, when compare to EOD training, but still it was interesting and extremely easy. My grades were very high and someone suggested that I look into EOD but I found it very difficult to follow through on.

When we graduated from school and our next duty assignments were posted I was very disappointed to find that being an enlistee or R.A. designation (regular Army) as opposed to the U.S. designation (draftee status), all the R.A. received orders for Germany, while the U.S. were given orders for Viet Nam.

This makes perfect sense in the military way of thinking because the draftee only served two years and after basic and schooling the Army was running out of time to put these men in-country. On the other hand the R.A. served three years so by sending them to Germany, the Army had a stock pile of ammo humpers to fall back on to fill slots in Viet Nam. But unlike most men, I didn't want to be stationed in Germany, I wanted to go to Viet Nam.

I complained to my First Sgt., a really nice man and he explained that getting my orders changed from Germany to Viet Nam would be difficult if not impossible. Then he asked if I had ever thought of going in to EOD and I admitted that I had but had found it difficult to get an interview.

Well, as it just happened, he had a good friend in EOD there on post and would give him a call if I so desired. I did so desire and he made the call. Strange thing this EOD field, I couldn't get them to consider me for their group until my First Sgt. called and within the hour I was sitting in front of a specially convened board just to judge me for their school.

I was accepted but I had to spend a few weeks of duty with the EOD team at Redstone while waiting for a slot to open up at the EOD School in Indian Head, Maryland. This duty was usually common labor cutting weeds with an idiot stick, or helping to set up problems for the EOD teams in that Army area who came there to be tested and recertified.

I worked for a Sgt. Starret, a good man, handy and knowledgeable about nearly everything. Those of us who were assigned to him watched his every move and we learned a great deal about explosives before starting school.

Sgt. Starret had a stiff index finger on his left hand, he seldom grasped anything with that finger using instead his middle finger or naughty finger or salute finger, or whatever you want to call it. In any case, we novices watched this man so intently that we began to catch ourselves not using our index finger. We would pick up a slice of bread leaving our index finger standing straight out, or we would grasp a set of key's or a wrench again with the index finger standing at attention. While this act became funny to us we began to spot other men who had worked for this famous Sergeant forgetting to use their index finger. I guess you could say the man left a permanent impression on us.

I then moved to Ft. McClelland at Anniston, Alabama for Chemical School. I had spent two weeks previously at this school for chemical classes while attending Ammunition School, however as you can imagine the EOD training was much more advanced and entertaining.

One reason for this, the EOD School classes were made up of all branches of the military from the rank of E-2 to Captains. It was unusual to be on the same footing with mid-rank NCO's and officers. Of this group only one Air Force Captain was a jerk who thought he was too good to attend class with common enlisted men and often made just such comments to the class members and the instructors, most of whom where enlisted men. This Captain would refuse to do many of the unpleasant programs in the schooling while the other officers and enlisted men took part good naturedly, realizing many of these exercises were inflicted as a test to see just how dedicated an individual was to becoming an EOD.

I first met Jim Poindexter at Ft. McClelland, he was an Air Force Sergeant and a truly good person. Jim became my mentor throughout EOD School. I give him credit for my being able to attend and finish EOD School. Jim was a savvy man who warned me on several occasions about unforeseen upcoming problems. He had a great sense of humor and a wealth of military information, having come from a large military family.

I found the EOD School challenging but not difficult, if you listened to the very fine instructors and studied several hours every night and on weekends. This extended study was necessary for most of us because of the thousands of items that we had to recall at a moment's notice. Plus each piece of ordnance had five to ten additional precautions or hazards that had to be memorized.

I found Conventional EOD School rewarding and even fun if you discount the fact that everyone there out-ranked me, so I was at the bottom of the barrel to some people but for the most part the instructors and students treated everyone equally.

After completing Conventional Ordnance School I was given orders to report to the 71st EOD at Clinton County Air Force Base just outside of Wilmington, Ohio. This was a very small reserve Air Force Base about three miles from Wilmington, neither of which anyone knew how to find.

When I tried to get airline tickets from Washington D.C. to Wilmington they could not figure out where it was located. I was flown to Columbus, Ohio where I changed planes for Dayton, Ohio, then I was scheduled to go by bus to Cincinnati, Ohio where I changed buses for the ride to Wilmington. The strange part to me was the fact that Wilmington is located inside of a triangle of these three large cities. In fact, the bus from Dayton to Cincinnati went with in a few miles of Wilmington. It would have been more convenient for all concerned if I had called the 71st from any of the three large cities and had them come there to pick me up.

This base was so small that we ate in a tiny mess hall with the officers and flight crews and for this reason the food was good; not quite as good as at Indian Head because it was a Navy School and those folks know how to serve good food.

This small base didn't provide much for its service people and even less for our Army detachment, in fact all of our records were kept at Ft. Knox, Kentucky. If one of us wanted or needed anything it had to go through Ft. Knox, communicated by telephone or letter. This was years before computers and fax machines.

I was fortunate that my Commanding Officer at the 71st was a young Capt. John Barbush who did his best to help his men. He got me promoted to E-4 so I could return to Indian Head to take the nuclear phase of the EOD School. After its competition I was promoted to E-5.

The 71st had the same fast roll-over in Senior NCO's and First Sergeants that we experienced in Viet Nam. Fact of the matter is, I never even met two of these First Sergeants I had that year and one of the others only stayed long enough to change our filling system to his system.

I found out that there is a standard in the Army for everything, like how your spare socks are to be rolled up and how your toothpaste tube had to lay just so but there is no set pattern for First Sergeants in EOD installing their own filling system. I didn't like the idea of sitting around night after night on what I considered was to be our time, (by this I mean the single men living in our EOD building while the married men went home) to sort and change these filing systems to whatever the new First Sgt. thought was the correct way. It was even more maddening when within a few weeks the First Sgt. would move on and a new man would take his place and immediately announce the old system didn't fit his way of thinking and it would have to be done over again, his way from the ground up.

At this point we had no free time because the EOD Unit had to know exactly where we were 24-7 or else we were considered a deserter, not AWOL with a 30 day grace period but a deserter. Desertion meant hard time up to and including the death sentence. No wonder I kept volunteering for Viet Nam.

The last First Sgt. I had at the 71st was not my cup of tea, we fought all the time, normally because of his strange rules and ideas. We had several yelling matches, mostly because I knew he was throwing away my forms where I volunteered for Viet Nam, which the Army frowned on. Finally during one of these heated debates Capt. Barbush could stand no more so he called Ft. Knox and asked them to send me to Viet Nam.

This 71st EOD Unit is where I met the late Dick Kornmann, the man who got my orders changed in-country for my assignment to the 3rd Herd. Dick was a true character and one of a kind. He always stood behind me whether in heated argument or a disagreement with the Army.

For some reason I thought leaving the 71st and moving on to the 3rd Herd would, in changing old friends and acquaintances, somehow change my luck. But Dick proved me wrong, I must thank him for all the practical jokes and dirty tricks that he played on me while we served together. Trying to stay ahead of him kept me on my toes and detecting unseen obstacles that might have prevented me from finishing my tour in-country.

GARY JAY POOL

MY HOME IN-COUNTRY

My in-country experience started by reporting to Ft. Lewis, Washington where we waited several days to be assigned a flight out. We departed from Ft. Lewis in the middle of the night, landing some six hours later in Anchorage with a beautiful winter sunrise.

This stop was very brief and we were soon back in the air aboard a four engine commercial jet whose body had been lengthened to haul more troops per flight. It could be a matter of perception but it seemed the seats were also closer together and the food was nonexistent for the 13 hour flight to Japan. From Japan to Cam Rahn Bay, South Viet Nam seemed a short hop after the long hours spent crossing the Pacific Ocean. The flight had originated in the dark of night in Washington State but from Anchorage we had flown in bright sun shine, finally arriving half way around the world in the middle of the afternoon. Talk about jet lag!

The flight home originated near midnight at Bien Hoa Air Base and landed in Okinawa at sunrise; the sunset was about four hours later.

We stopped in Hawaii in the dark and landed in Oakland, California at sunrise. The flight over was in all daylight while the return trip had to be endured thru the long dark night. This made for an uncomfortable ride for me as I had become used to registering land marks while flying around in-country but there was nothing to see high over the middle of the Pacific in the middle of the night.

I had been offered the opportunity to go by ship to Viet Nam which was reported to take 21 days off of my time in-country but I declined. I was in too much of a hurry to get in-country to waste my time on a pleasure cruise. However, I will admit that I often had second thoughts about my rapid decision to go by air.

Upon arriving at Cam Rahn Bay we were nearly overcome by the searing heat of the day; something that we were not accustomed to coming from winter in the states. We were formed up and marched down the street to a tent with long rows of tin troughs where we were told to brush our teeth. I never knew the reason for this exercise other than the cadre could not deal with our bad morning breath after the long flight.

We were then instructed in the use of sun screen and insect repellant (neither of which were available to us throughout our tour in-country) not to mention the hazards of the many varieties of dangerous critters indigenous to

Southeast Asia. Our group was given the typical Army bums rush being moved from point A to point B for some fabricated pretense just to keep everyone busy. There were never any real answers as to what or where we went. Suddenly we were told to grab our gear and prepare to be loaded on a plane to be sent south. The ride was a C-130 cargo plane and the southern destination proved to be Bien Hoa Air Base.

We GI's were loaded on the C-130 thru the rear tail gate and told to take a seat on the hard metal deck that served as the main floor. Just before take-off a group of South Vietnamese civilians were brought aboard and were directed to the canvas web seats that lined the plane's exterior walls. It was interesting to note that these civilian's carry-on baggage consisted of pigs, chickens, and a couple of small goats.

The big C-130 backed out of its protective revetment then lumbered up and down the runway a couple of times before finally gaining enough velocity to break the law of gravity. I thought it odd that the plane's crew chief waited until the very last moment to close the rear loading ramp. But it wasn't long before the tropical heat and the close confinement of the planes interior combined to release odors from the on-board livestock that only a sewage plant worker could love. I knew then that the crew chief had left the tail gate down in a futile effort to maintain a well ventilated aircraft for as long as possible.

The big old cargo plane lumbered and jumped and bucked across the clear Asian sky for what seemed hours to my butt's way of thinking. We were originally told this would be a short flight but then it was reported that storms lay in our path so we had to change course. After a time I became envious and then resentful towards the local civilians whose animals were resting semi-peacefully in the much more comfortable web seats.

The flight continued on and on before it occurred to me that either we were flying in circles or South Viet Nam was a larger country than I thought. Of course, it could have been we were on a very slow air plane, which made me glad that C-130's were not used to transport troops from the states to Nam.

We finally set down on the runway at Bien Hoa Air Force Base and no one had to tell us twice to exit the plane; of course that happened only after the civilians and livestock had leisurely deplaned. This was my first experience with the Asian lifestyle which proved to be much slower and more casual than anything in the states. The adjustment came easily to some GI's while others never fully accepted the relaxed, timeless attitude of the natives.

At Bien Hoa the C-130 was met by military buses that rushed us to the 90th replacement depot at Long Binh. This establishment proved to be another exercise in controlled confusion. It was here that I was warned that I might not be assigned to an EOD unit. It was here that I warned them if I was not assigned to an EOD unit there would be hell to pay. Perhaps this is not the proper military attitude but then I never claimed to have the proper military attitude. The Army had cried and begged for EOD men to come to Viet Nam and I had volunteered repeatedly and fought like hell to get in-country so I had no intention of being stuck in some ammo company. I felt certain if I were wrongly placed, simply making contact with any EOD unit would immediately rectify the problem.

At the replacement depot life seemed to stand still. I thoroughly disliked such companies, they were so unsettled. I couldn't wait to be assigned nearly anywhere in order to escape the ever-moving sea of green fatigues of the new replacements. We were forced to endure days of limbo waiting to learn our fate.

One might think that a post is a post but there can be a great deal of difference from base to base and job to job in places like South Viet Nam. The luck of the draw might land one man in a tent compound that was nothing but a tiny mud hole in the middle of nowhere, while another man with the same M.O.S. might very well find his place in a nice barracks, with a good mess hall and a big post exchange next door.

The common GI's idle mind is a playground for a fertile imagination, which in a replacement company keeps the air filled with ridiculous rumors and false scuttlebutt. No matter what orders a man might receive there are those who are willing to recount the horror and danger of that base. These tales usually originate with those who have never been in-country before, let alone have any first-hand experience with the subject at hand. Many men take these erroneous reports as the gospel truth and become so upset that they dream up schemes to avoid the duty. The permanent parties of these replacement companies who probably have never been to these dangerous bases often make matters worse for the young impressionable GI's by reinforcing the distressing myths. The replacement companies were also famous for fights and the theft of anything not nailed down. Needless to say I could hardly wait for orders to whatever fate Uncle Sam had prepared for me.

ASSIGNED TO THE 3RD ORD

The intense February sun beat down unmercifully on me as I sat in uncertainty on a bench just outside one of the 90th replacement company's buildings. I had just entered Viet Nam 36 hours before at glorious Cam Rahn Bay. I now was biding my time waiting for orders to be typed that would send me to Pleiku far to the north of Cam Rahn Bay.

"Typical military," I thought to myself, sending me down south so that I could go back up north. But I had little time to ponder the wisdom of the green machine for there was a whole new world unfolding around me that first real day in-country. I noticed right away that my shiny dark OD jungle fatigues set me apart from the more experienced troops whose faded dull uniforms and worn jungle boots were worn like a badge of distinction. This green-horn image was noticeable not only by the GI's but also by the Vietnamese who laughed at us after making disparaging remarks to one another in their native language.

Suddenly in the distance a string of powerful explosions ripped thru the hot humid late afternoon air drawing everyone's attention.

"EOD team," one of the GI's clad in very faded fatigues said nonchalantly to no one in particular.

"Have your orders ready in just a minute," the clerk inside the building behind me called out thru a battered screen door. He had, like everyone else rushed to see where the explosion originated.

"Good," I replied weakly, wishing I had been with the EOD team that had just set off the attention-attracting shots.

The troops in the area quickly returned to performing their everyday tasks as the excitement of the explosion waned and was soon forgotten. Forgotten by everyone but me, for I have always been drawn to explosives in any form. This fascination with anything that goes boom has been in my blood since I was just a child. I have always been intrigued by anything from fire crackers to nuclear weapons and this afternoon was no different.

A combination of envy, curiosity and boredom drew me from my seat in the sun to a nearby narrow blacktop street where I hoped for a better view of the demolition area. As I moved to the edge of the road, a fast moving Army jeep sailed by, locked up its brakes and slid to a stop.

It was then that I recognized the jeeps red fenders and emergency lights denoting it as an EOD vehicle. The unseen driver suddenly began backing up only to slide to a second stop directly in front of where I stood. The driver was a man I'll call Dick, his passenger was named Dave, both of whom I had known back in the world (as the U.S. was referred to). Although I wore no EOD insignia, Dick recognized me as he sped by.

"What are you doing?" he called out.

I explained I was waiting for orders to go north. My reply lit a fire under Sergeant Dick. He pulled his jeep off the road and raced inside the building as if the devil were after him. It was amazing to watch Sergeant Dick as he descended like a duck on a June bug on the replacement company's young clerk. Dick was a large man who seldom took no for an answer and no matter how much the clerk refused; he insisted that my orders be changed. The men of this building were totally unprepared for the sudden attack that consisted of a combination of rapid speech, odd reasoning, threats, cajoling, and he was not about to take no for an answer.

The next thing I knew my duffel bag and I were in the back of the 3rd Ord jeep headed for Long Binh Post. On the ride I learned my new First Sergeant was one of the toughest NCO's in the military. A hurried drive thru the countryside brought us to the famous Long Binh Post. We drove past the entrance to the Army's massive ammunition dump and turned in at a guarded gate at the edge of a grove of rubber trees. The 3rd Ord EOD building sat about a block from the main road surrounded by these tall evenly spaced ancient rubber trees.

Now, I was raised in dilapidated tenet houses usually on dead end dirt roads so I was far from accustomed to a luxurious lifestyle, but my first view of the 3rd Ord's EOD office/barracks was a true shock. I had seen many broken down farms with better hog houses than this structure. Actually it was very reminiscent of a beachcomber's shack or the shelter one might build of junk salvage from the sea when marooned on a deserted island. In fact, that is very nearly the case for the roof was corrugated tin, the walls were plywood and screen wire. OD colored sand bags were stacked three feet high against the building's exterior walls in a futile effort to protect those within. I suspect that whoever held the contract to supply sand bags to Viet Nam made more money than any other contractor. Ninety five percent of U.S. buildings in-country had just such green sandbags adorning the exterior, not counting all the bunkers and shelters that were completely covered with sandbags. The wet tropical climate took a heavy toll on these bags whether made of canvas or woven plastic. It was not unusual in the midst of torrential monsoon rains for one or more of these sandbag walls to collapse with a roar.

In the 3rd Ord Battalion area this roar was often followed a few seconds later by the detonation of a hand grenade. It seems the drug dealers and users, of which there were many, found the sandbag walls an ideal place to hide their illicit stashes. The hand grenades were placed, pin pulled, lever held secure by the sandbags as an unseen security system. (but getting off subject) A small porch and open doorway marked the entrance to the office where the unit's top NCO sat peering out at his returning jeep.

"Come on," Dick declared in a positive voice while parking the jeep, "Top Sgt. is at his desk so this is a good chance for you to meet him."

I grabbed my duffel bag and followed Dick and Dave thru the door to the desk occupied by a very stern faced Master Sergeant.

"Good evening Master Jack," Dick called out in his most charming voice, "here's your new EOD man, worked with him in the states."

"But we haven't got a man coming," came Master Jack's firm objection.

"We got one now," Dick smiled, stepping out another office door. "I'm late for chow," he announced quickly disappearing from sight, leaving Dave and I to explain how I come to be assigned to the unit that didn't need or want me.

As consequences of my unexpected arrival, I spent the next two weeks policing up cigarette butts and polishing spittoons until the powers-that-be decided I was fit for EOD incidents.

Blast cloud from demolition

EOD team at work

DESTINED TO BE IN
THE 3RD ORD

During this process of transferring stations I was given the opportunity to go to Viet Nam by ship. It was explained to me that this boat ride would be a 21 day reprieve from duty in-country. I declined, fearing I would spend 21 days as a deck hand or moving freight in some hot cargo hold. I now regret not accepting the offer to cross the Pacific Ocean by ship; still I fear I would not have been assigned to the 3rd Ord if my timing had not been prefect. It may sound foolish but I always felt destined to be in the 3rd Ord and really never wanted to transfer to any other unit in-country.

I don't believe man is important enough to be a piece to some grand mystical plan that predestines the fate of each of us, on the other hand I feel that win, lose or draw I must play out the hand that was dealt to me. In this case the 3rd Ord was the cards dealt to me and I thank God for it. I was fortunate to meet some of the best men I will ever know during my time at the 3rd and I also know that without these good understanding men I might have failed as a soldier and EOD man.

In summation I must state that my all too short experience with the EOD program was a great experience. I have always been intrigued in the mechanical workings of ordnance and that, combined with a keen interest in explosives, provided enough incentive to keep me out of serious trouble.

I willingly admit now that the only punishment I feared in the Army was that I might lose my EOD badge for one of my many indiscretions. I never seemed to quite fit the military mold but fortunately those around me were conscious of that fact. I always said to do EOD work a person had to be smart enough to do the job but not smart enough to know better. Nearly every EOD man I met fit those specifications perfectly. Many people have asked me why anyone with any sense would volunteer to disarm explosive ordnance. The only way that I can answer that is to state how many times the members of the 3rd Ord fought for the right to go on a bomb call. Big John, Tex, Junior and I were especially annoying to our clerk who often gave out the assignments. Dick was very efficient at dispatching the proper team to a particular situation. We may have done our best to persuade the man to send us on calls but he always won any ensuing argument.

The 3rd Ord was located in

a rubber tree grove

Our jeep with red lights & sirens

GARY JAY POOL

FRAGGINGS

I have often stated that during my tour of duty in Viet Nam I was fortunate enough to meet and work with some of the finest men I have ever known. Oh, there were a number to slackers, goldbrickers, bums, and druggies in the mix, but for the most part the men and women of the U.S. military performed their assigned tasks with little regard for their personal safety or comfort. These people never expected and seldom received accolades or rewards for the services they performed daily without fail.

I was even more fortunate than the average soldier for I was part of a ten man EOD team. I blundered into the 3rd Ordnance Battalion EOD at Long Binh Post completely by accident and I remained there throughout my tour in-country. That being the proper name for the unit, it was usually referred to as the 3rd Herd. This title was self-inflicted and self-perpetuated partially because we were less than a strike or spit and polished military unit. The Herd not only pushed the envelope as they say, we looked for a different path, we were trying, as the hippies used say, "to find ourselves." Some of the other EOD units were just as disreputable as the Herd but we had somehow accumulated a number of characters who lent a certain notorious air to the units reputation.

These EOD units had little or no drug problem with their members, but it was a different story in our billeting areas. Drug activities, green on green violence and deadly fragging's were the rule rather than the exception.

Fragging is a term used to describe one soldiers attempt to kill another soldier or group of soldiers with an explosive device. Because of the explosive device employed in such incidents, the EOD teams were called to assist in the investigation. The fragging incidents ranged from humorous to ones with horrible injuries and death. Our job was to disarm any explosive device or if a detonation had occurred, to determine what ordinance had been employed.

These fragging's could come anytime day or night with officers and high ranking NCO being the favorite target. After a time you learn that fragging calls from a certain area would usually be fake or a practical joke being played on someone of authority by a disgruntled drug user. Still, all calls had to be taken seriously, because most of them were real life-threatening events. Case in point, drug dealers would scout around and find one of the old MK 2 hand grenades that have a heavy steel body cast in squared lugs.

The operation of this weapon entails holding the grenade in the throwing hand with the lever or spoon tucked in tight against the web of the thumb, then you pull the pin with the offhand and throw at the target. While traveling through the air, a spring flips off the lever which has been holding down a striker. The striker snaps over, impacting a primer which lights a time delay of four to seven seconds before the main charge, TNT detonates. The military also produced several training versions of these grenades that didn't explode, some just popped while others didn't have levers that flipped off. This type of hand grenade or one of its successors that had smooth bodies were the choice of these fraggers.

Now to change subjects for a minute and explain that most of the barracks or hooches as they were called in Viet Nam were basically a shed that was built on the ground with plywood floors. The dimensions varied but were oblong in shape maybe twenty by forty feet with one screen door on each end. The walls were plywood half way up with screen wire filling the top half. Sand bags were stacked against the four-foot plywood walls to prevent shrapnel from penetrating inside the building. The roofs were made of tin with a pitch to shed the intense monsoon rains.

Now here's the picture: plywood flooring, only two exits, bunks spaced evenly across the floor in the open bay style, no room dividers. So now we have the recipe for the perfect fragging. The weapon a hand grenade. The target: a make-shift building filled with sleeping GIs. The scene: a very dark night, no exterior lighting due to black-out regulations. The players; one or two disgruntled drugged up soldiers. Action: one actor opens the screen door while the second one rolls a hand grenade down the center of the hooch.

The heavy lugs on the rolling pineapple grenade makes a distinct tattoo sound as they contact the plywood flooring. The buildings lights are out. In the dark only the sense of earing is fully functioning when someone yells grenade and all hell breaks loose. Men are jumping from their bunks, each one racing for one of the two doors in their underwear as they trip over bunks and gear, not to mention colliding with one another. A traffic jam develops at both doors and driven by panic, some poor soul tries to dive head first through one of the screen wire walls. The attempt fails of course, but the soldier will be branded with a strange rash on his head for several days.

If the grenade does detonate the EOD team is called in to aid in the investigation. We search through the destruction, blood and possibly bodies to determine what type of device was employed and where it came from.

If the grenade didn't detonate the EOD team carefully enters the building hoping this particular device is an inert practice grenade, while at the same time praying the unexploded grenade is not a dud with a hung striker or mechanical impairment.

Those who survive these mock fragging's show injuries like broken toes, bloody noses, black eyes or little checkered marks from rubbing their skin against screen wire.

Often times these incidents were perpetrated by drugged up soldiers using practice grenades hoping to get even with some NCO, by either scaring him half to death, or by showing him up for a coward. No matter the results in either case the criminals involved were usually hiding at a safe distance enjoying the fruits of their handy work.

This all sounds like a joke but it was a serious matter to the occupants of the hooch and the EOD team, not to mention the emergency personnel who responded to such incidents.

As I have said, these fragging's were less common in broad daylight so we were surprised at being called to a Long Binh Engineer Battalion, an area that we were not very familiar with. I say it was not a very familiar area because the engineer outfits were usually made up of good hard working men who, being schooled in explosives, often handled their own problems. The place and the time of day peaked our interest so we were ready for anything upon arrival. However, the detonation had already taken place before we were notified, so we merely investigated the incident and searched the area for any other clandestine explosive device.

In this particular case some unhappy soldier had placed a U.S. Claymore mine with its back to a steel conex box then aimed the device at the corner of a wooden building approximately ten feet away. The target inside the building was the desk of an officer who fortunately had moved just before the Claymore detonated. The force of the blast moved the heavy conex box several feet while the shrapnel from the directional mine caused severe damage to the building.

We reported our findings then returned to our building never knowing if the perpetrator was ever caught or how the officer felt knowing that someone in his unit wanted him dead.

COMPANY CLERK

Many of the urgent calls we received were from young inexperienced officers who had no idea of the ordnance they were dealing with. A typical telephone call from some distraught Second Lieutenant would consist of a lot of excited jabbering with words like "Emergency, Urgent, Sudden Death, The world ending immediately, or GET YOUR BUTT OVER HERE AND THAT'S AN ORDER!"

The first problem with this scenario being that a non-qualified EOD, NCO or officer was restricted from giving us a direct order concerning the handling or render safe procedure or the operations of our units. The older and wiser noncoms and officers called with the information needed to mount a proper response, knowing full well we loved nothing better than to answer a call for help. It was what we lived for, even to the point of heated arguments among the men as to who would be allowed to take the call. We were like little kids fighting over a toy or a piece of candy.

Our clerk, Dick Hause had the innate ability of quickly settling these childish disagreements, usually to everyone's mutual satisfaction. He easily managed the unit's day to day operations, while completing his own work. The man had a great sense of our area and how to get from place to place, he usually knew every man's location, who they were teamed with that day, the weak and strong suits of that combination, and whether a team could be easily contacted by radio.

Dick manned the radio and the telephone 24 hours a day in an attempt to keep us out of harm's way. He also had the ability to capture the importance of the everyday happenings and verbally express them in a clear concise sentence.

I believe that the one quality EOD men and many other people who passed through the 3rd Ord will remember most about Dick was his unwavering smile. The man wore an infectious friendly grin even in his sleep. Always the first to offer help, that kindly facial expression carried over into every act of Dick's daily life.

But one of Dick's most valuable assets came to the front when he answered phone calls from hot-headed, verbally abusive people who feared the piece of ordnance in question had the destructive power of a hydrogen bomb. Dick had a great working knowledge of ordnance and their inherent dangers. The man never got belligerent with excited threatening callers but kept a polite sunny disposition to all who called the 3rd Ord EOD unit for assistance.

The one unfaltering component was Dick Hause's steady hand on our control. He was well established at the 3rd Ord long before my arrival and was there long after I departed. In my eleven months with the 3rd Herd we had five Commanding Officers and six First Sergeants but only one clerk.

Dick remained a steadfast friend to all, through the good and the bad, without a complaint. He was and is a true member of the 3rd Herd. Thanks You, Dick !

MORTAR FLARE PROJECTILE

It was not unusual to drive across post with red lights flashing and sirens wailing in response to a possible fragging or booby trap call only to find a handful of deteriorating rifle cartridges that had brought the whole area to a standstill because the person in charge had over-reacted to the hazards involved. The thought of just leaving the items undisturbed never seemed to occur to these people.

One of the common panic calls came in the form of expended mortar flare projectiles. The mortar flare is a very well thought-out and highly useful piece of ordnance that consists of a flare and parachute that are loaded into a cylinder body with a fuse on one end and stabilizing fins on the other end. When the mortar shell is fired it travels in a high arching trajectory, somewhere in this pathway the preset nose fuse functions which causes a separation of the stabilizing fins. The parachute and flare are drug out of the steel tube-like body, the nose and tail pieces fall to earth while the parachute and flare float slowly down, giving off a brilliant light.

Because the spent shell of the mortar may fall within our perimeter or in some unusual place many think these are dud-fired shells or ones that have been converted for fragging or booby traps. The empty metal tubes are often confused with a short round which is a projectile whose propellant for whatever reason, did not push it out past our lines to the enemy target. These short rounds if unexploded can be dangerous to military personnel and do require disposal operations.

However, usually only a cursory inspection even from a safe distance will differentiate between a short round and an expended flare. The expended flare body is nothing but a hollow steel tube with no hazard potential other than it hurts to drop one on your foot. Many men, including EOD men have received medals for doing nothing more than picking up and disposing of a completely safe steel tube. Just another example of how poorly trained and inexperienced our armed forces were in Viet Nam and how panic-stricken some men become in the presence of explosives.

NEVER SAFE FROM HARM

As I have described before, many hooches, bunkers and basically all buildings were protected by sand bags. The original bags were manufactured from canvas while the later units were constructed of green plastic. It was hoped the plastic variety would better withstand the rot and natural state of decay that was present year around in Viet Nam. I have no evidence that the transition was any improvement, however I do believe the drug dealers found the new bags an improvement over the canvas type.

Why just the drug dealers you might ask? Answer, they liked to hide their drug stash in these sandbag walls for protection. No, not from the monsoon rains but from other soldiers, or dealers who might steal their investments. They would lift up the end of a sand bag, then place their drugs underneath and as far back as possible, then the druggy would place a hand grenade under the sand bag in such a way as to use the weight of the sandbag to hold the spoon in place. Then with everything set, the druggy would pull the fuse's safety pin, thus arming the grenade with a total disregard for the lives of the unsuspecting soldiers or Vietnamese in the area.

During the heavy monsoon rains, the sandbag walls would deteriorate and eventually collapse with a roaring sound. When this sound of rushing water filled the air, the savvy veteran would dive for cover, or if inside a building, drop to the floor to await the inevitable detonation.

Drug dealers were seldom punished for their illegal activity. Even when caught red-handed in possession of contraband items, most of the time they were asked if the material was theirs, to which they would naturally say no. For some reason that gave them a free pass. The US Army often turned a blind eye to the drug problem.

We had men killed and injured while serving on main bases by these thoughtlessly placed druggy alarms. So never let it be said that a soldier who is not out in the jungle was safe from harm, many a man was injured or killed by our own soldiers right on base.

DEADLY DET CORD

One particular incident that I will never forget had some of the traits of a fragging but more than likely it was due to improper training.

It was late afternoon when my partner and I were just coming back on post from a long hot day of inspecting a Viet Cong arms cache. We had to check several hundred pieces of captured Russian and Chinese ordnance, explosive handmade mines and booby traps to certify they were safe to handle or destroy. We were covered in dirt and wet with sweat which was the uniform of the day in-country for most soldiers. We were hungry and exhausted as we cleared the south gate of Long Binh post when our Jeep radio crackled on with a message from our clerk, Dick Hause to divert to another call. This was not unusual, missing meals or sleep was SOP or standard operating procedure in all EOD units around the world and as we were often told, eating or sleeping at regular hours was the life of a civilian.

Dick had little information on the call other than a detonation had occurred in what was thought to be inside the ammo dump, a scenario that makes all EOD personnel's hair stand on end. We followed the instructions for locating the incident sight, an area we were poorly acquainted with.

Our directions led us to a large metal building just outside the ammo dump wire, a fact we considered a plus. We were expected and quickly directed to the explosion site. A number of fatigue-clad soldiers were standing around what appeared to be a class or training exercise. This was a bad mistake on the part of those in charge. The area should have been cleared of non-essential personnel immediately to prevent the possibility of injuries if a second explosion should occur as was often the case.

The scene was unusual in that in the middle of the floor sat the remains of a steel 55 gallon drum, a man's body being hurriedly evacuated plus a lot of nervous soldiers. My partner that day, was an accomplished detective, a very necessary skill in bomb disposal. He quickly discerned from the material scattered about the site what had taken place before anyone stepped forward to give us the pertinent information.

At this point a very nervous NCOIC or non-commissioned officer in charge stepped forward to explain what had taken place. It seems the unit was having a training class given by another NCO who was explaining the use of detonating cord, its safe handling and disposal.

Detonating cord or det cord, the subject of this incident is usually a plastic tube filled with a high explosive that is used to transfer or continue a detonation wave. A lot of the det cord we used looked very much like the white plastic clothes line rope from the sixties and seventies but it can be red or green or any color your heart desires. Det cord is a wonderful and safe tool in the hands of well-trained personnel but can be very dangerous when mishandled. But it has become a military legend, ex-soldiers repeat fables of the super natural destructive powers attributed to this wonder cord.

I have been regaled with hundreds of tales of someone clearing a whole forest of trees with one wrap of det cord or how someone cut a vehicle in half with a few coils of the wondrous line. I'll be the first to admit having unlimited access to det cord and plenty of time to experiment. We tried every movie scenario and found most of them to be someone's daydream or bar room bragging. Most of these exaggerated tales came up short of the reported effectiveness of det cord.

But you must give the devil his due, det cord is a powerful deadly explosive that has enhanced the world of blasting and at the same time made such work safer for the personnel involved.

In this particular case it was obvious that the instructor teaching the class did not know his subject matter thoroughly. As I said, my partner quickly pieced together the puzzle, because laying on the ground near the burn barrel was a military issue demolition pack. These demo bags contained plastic explosive, time fuse, fuse lighter and sensitized det cord. This sensitized det cord had non-electric blasting caps crimped on the ends. In other words, the pouch contained everything needed to set off a very respectable explosion while operating in the field. However, it broke all the rules for safe handling of explosives that was taught and so stringently enforced by the military around the world. This segregation is done mainly by how sensitive an explosive is and its function. Since non-electric blasting caps contain an explosive that is sensitive to heat, flame and impact, it is kept at a safe distance from plastic, TNT, or dynamite explosives to prevent accidents. But here they were all bundled in one convenient package, one that all EOD men handled with great respect. In this case, the class instructor removed the det cord with the blasting caps crimped in place then deposited them in the fire thinking this was a safe and proper disposal.

The result: the fire set off the blasting caps, which in turn detonated the coil of det cord, tearing the barrel apart and removing the instructor's legs. We later received a message that the man died as a result of his injuries.

Nearly everyone makes mistakes on the job and explosive handling is no different than any other profession but it is a very unforgiving occupation when you do make a mistake. We never knew if the instructor knew better than to place blasting caps in the fire, or if he was not familiar with this demo pouch and thought he was merely destroying time fuse. Whatever the reason, it was a tragic waste of life for no purpose.

Although weary and dirty we made a full inspection and reported our findings as we felt it necessary to perform in a professional manner, while there wasn't much we could do except to explain over and over to those shocked personnel present what they had witnessed. Most of these men had never witnessed a man perish under such a violent circumstance, especially a man they knew in what should have been a relatively safe environment, if there is such a place in a war zone.

PACKAGE FROM HOME

In a world where death and dismemberment is your stock and trade, life (theirs and sometimes your own) becomes a cheap commodity. Witnessing a person being killed in whatever manner becomes mundane to the average soldier. Most soldiers accept death as part of war, you might say it's how the belligerent sides keep score, but some soldiers begin to enjoy these events even to the point of finding humor in the fatal act. These people should be avoided like the plaque.

Fortunately the American troops for the most part found little reward in taking lives and for the most part are truly sympathetic to the loss of life. But many soldiers must find a stress relief. Many drink, some do drugs while others find a hobby.

Now this may sound ridiculous but the average soldier is very resourceful when it comes to entertaining oneself. Reading is quite common, photography and writing, especially letters to home or reading and rereading letters from loved ones gave personnel a sense they were still part of the world back home.

During the Viet Nam War communication with the world was non-existent except by mail. Oh, there were occasions in times of extreme emergency when the military would connect up with ham operators around the globe to get a message home. The mail could take a week to ten days or longer to deliver a letter, and sometimes the said letter never arrived.

I can state from personal experience that I had more than one package from home become lost. One was in a plane crash and I was told it was a complete loss. A couple of months later the package arrived all battered, crumpled and dirty but still intact. It was full of goodies, brownies that were hard as bullets, candy that was dried out and a cake that resembled a pancake.

You might say my parents were very accomplished packers. On receiving this package, I took it to the day-room as was our custom, to share with all my teammates. They were not quite sure whether to chance eating the always longed-for luxuries but after some brownies were hammered on the table and thrown against the wall, it was decided to make a few experiments on what might make these treats more palatable. It was quickly decided that in the world of EOD, beer went with everything, so beer as usual became the answer.

Beer had long since been considered the gift of the Gods in the EOD world, the thinking being that the amber liquid could promote healing, cure illnesses, preserve your manhood and it wasn't bad to cook with either. But no matter its application, beer was the answer and in the case of the battered care-package, once lavishly applied as a sauce or as a dip, the aged goodies quickly disappeared. In my next letter home I relayed messages of thank you from my team members, all of whom prayed for another package and many of the crew suggested that my parents would be well advised to beat and kick the package before it was shipped.

On a serious note, I had a favorite uncle and grandmother pass away while in-country. The only notice in each case was a delayed letter from home. They were both laid to rest before I knew of their passing, I couldn't send flowers or even a card for the military had made no provisions for such an event.

The military did provide one television station and one radio station, both of which were heavily censured as to truth and content. Reading material available to the common GI left much to be desired. I knew of the My Lai massacre before the average soldier only because packages sent by my parents from home were always padded with current newspapers and magazines. Of course, the word of the killings eventually leaked out from new personnel in-country and those returning from R&R.

One of the true highlights of the day was the seemingly mundane mail call and yet for many it was the highlight of the day. Happy, excited men were the rule rather than the exception but many soldiers turned away misty eyed. They walked with a defeated shuffle knowing another day had passed without a word from home and loved ones. Those who couldn't read or write (and there were many) often skipped mail call if possible hoping to avoid heartache and embarrassment. The anti-war sentiment in the United States ran so deep in some families their sons were shunned for allowing themselves to be drafted rather than leave the country.

I knew one man who had been an ardent anti-war protester before the war; he was drafted and rather than break the law, reported for induction. This led to his family completely disowning him, they stopped all communication with him, plus his fiancé broke off their engagement.

This young man had drawn a large peace symbol on his helmet's canvas cover, not an unusual declaration but since we had to work with him under arms, there was some doubt in our minds. But he performed his duties as required to the point that we trusted him as much or more than many of the soldiers we relied on for security. When his tour in-country was nearly over and he reached that longed-for short timer status, we made a point to say good bye, shake his hand and wish him well. As we talked, I asked him what life back in the world held for him after being disowned by friends and family. He answered good naturedly but not apologetically that he intended to let his hair grow long while painting protest signs and he would find a place to demonstrate against the war. I believe the young soldier knowing full well my commitment to the war, thought he would get a rise out of me. Instead I told him I thought his intentions were honorable and I could think of no one more qualified to protest the war than one who had lived through a year of it. We parted friends that day, while sharing a difference of opinion knowing we would never meet again. But I held a great respect for this man and the thousands of men just like him who answered their countries call to arms even though in their hearts they felt it wrong.

GRAVES REGISTRATION STANDOFF

Many service personnel can define the time of day by breakfast, dinner, or supper. Chow time is a very important time reference to most people except emergency personnel like EOD. Our meal and sleep times, especially in Viet Nam, were never scheduled or regimented as is the practice of the regular military. We ate and slept at odd hours or not at all, a common occurrence.

I state this only as an explanation that this incident started sometime after breakfast which I had missed and before noon. A phone call came in requesting our services at the flight line at Can Tho Base situated down in the Delta. Lack of reported information by the caller left us, as usual, with no firm plan of operation other than three of our team had to hurry to the Medivac Hospital to catch a helicopter flight.

The uneventful flight in one of the workhorse Huey helicopters was as usual an enjoyable interlude and a time for quiet thought.

An explosion on the flight line was the only current information as to what lay ahead, but being uninformed was an everyday situation. This meant you could not prepare your mind for any particular situation, or try to remember how a particular fuse worked. Flexibility and adaptability were a routine commodity in bomb disposal.

When the Huey sat down on the hot concrete we unloaded through the side door, allowing us to see another Huey helicopter far down the runway, nose and tail touching the ground, it's back broken near the jet engine. It was truly a sad picture, something akin to a broken down old Calvary horse, its head hanging low awaiting the pistol shot that would end its misery.

Thinking this old war bird was our objective, we headed down the long concrete strip expecting to find some hazardous ordnance contained within the aircrafts dark ominous olive drab body. This looked like an easy call and we had taken only a few steps before being diverted off the runway to an area cordoned off by a disheveled mass of chain link fence. This we were unceremoniously told was our project for the day.

The area in question was a mountain of metal rubble, wooden shipping blocks and God only knows what else would be found hidden in the accumulated debris. Questioning just what had happened and what explosives might be present met with some resistance but eventually the truth came out. It seems the fenced-in area was a small ammo storage area, its contents were questionable at best, even though the military has strict rules and guidelines for handling and storage of explosives and hazardous material.

I had attended ammunition storage school before volunteering for EOD training and it took only a quick glance around to decide this was not an approved storage area. However, this was not out of the norm in Viet Nam, as many field expedience or shortcuts were put in place for the benefit of the using troops. We did not consider ourselves a policing unit so we normally left such irregularities, unless insanely dangerous, to the powers that be.

The other half of the story was slow to be revealed, it seems a metal conex box full of high explosives had been placed just outside the make-shift depot gate. The heavy metal door of the container had been left open and a soldier was seated on top in a metal lawn chair trying to soak up the tropical sun. Far down the runway a Huey crew was down-loading a 2.75 inch rocket pod. Suddenly one of the rockets static fired for whatever reason, then raced down the runway and into the open conex box door. The 2.75 rocket's high explosive warhead detonated, setting off the explosives stored in the metal cube plus some of the ordnance in the storage area.

Naturally that huge explosion completely disassemble the poor GI who had regrettably picked the top of the conex box as a prime place to get a tan. At this point we were prevented from entering the storage area until Graves Registration was on the scene. We occupied our time by searching for the remains of the sun-bathing soldier. We did find both of his feet still inside of his jungle boots, his wallet and his head, the remainder of his body was scattered about the blast sight.

Tired of the delay and having recovered the larger pieces of the body, we headed into the rubble to begin performing render-safe procedures to make the area safe for others to enter, notably the men from Graves Registration. Upon their arrival we were informed their party would not enter the hazardous area, however regulations prohibited anyone else from collecting any of the dead soldier's body parts.

As I have stated time and again, I believe that cleaning up any ammunition storage area after it has experienced a detonation is the most hazardous operation an EOD team can perform. There is no way of knowing the condition of the explosives, if the fuses are armed or not, and just what lies hidden where one false step might trigger another and possibly larger detonation.

So we were at a standoff, the Graves Registration team with their shoulder length see-through plastic gloves and three feet long tweezers refused to enter the blast area while at the same time refusing to let us do our work. Needless to say a heated argument ensued as they quoted regulations and we noted common sense.

Our team that day was made up of a Staff Sergeant, a Spec 4 and myself, a Spec 5 but as I have said many times, rank meant very little in EOD at that time. A team member was expected to perform his duty in a professional manner no matter his rank. My teammates that day were my dear friends and unfortunately they are gone now, both men were known for their cool heads and vast experience in bomb disposal and a great working knowledge of the ordnance at hand. And while they were good friends, they were nearly exact opposites in personality. So as usual in bomb disposal, a conference was called to determine the best way to handle this situation.

I am amazed that people think these little meetings were hostile or that the highest ranking man made the final decision because nothing could be farther from the truth. We were on a team, one like so many others operated with great respect for the other members. The older man was known for his laid back approach, the younger man was known as a big man with physical straight-forward mannerism. I held the rank in the middle, well let's say I was known to be brash and hot headed, always one to take charge and let the chips fall where they may.

Finally I turned and walked directly into the devastated ammo dump and began working on the task at hand. The explosives and rocket motor bodies were covered with long strips of what looked like burned crispy bacon but in reality this flesh was the remains of the sunbathing soldier. The team from Graves Registration began to yell their objections to my actions while telling our Staff Sergeant to order me out of the area. You can imagine how far that went when I knew they were terrified to enter the area and I was immediately joined by my team members.

We carefully and respectfully removed any and all material from the dead man's body, placed them in a plastic bag using our bare hands which drew howls of protest from the Graves Registration team. However, it's very difficult to do a RSP on many pieces of explosive ordnance with cumbersome and slick plastic gloves on your hands.

With the mission complete and all explosives rendered safe we withdrew from the area with the warning there would be complaints filed and repercussion forth coming. But there are many occasion in a war zone where the rulebook isn't applicable, and I'll bet the average in-country EOD unit broke as many or more of these ridiculous regulations as anyone.

As for the repercussions, they were quickly rendered, duly noted and just as quickly forgotten.

CHINOOK RIDE

Speaking of disregarding regulations, as we finished clearing the ammo depot at Can Tho the three of us began to wonder about transportation back to Long Binh. As was often the case, no one at our unit had made any arrangements for our return. This was pretty standard operating procedure at the 3rd Ord, when out on a job no one had made arrangements for us to eat at the mess halls or to find sleeping quarters, we were expected to live by our wits. I asked the men who had requested our services but they had no idea of how or where we could make connections for return transportation. Finally one soldier stated that a Chinook helicopter had just landed farther up the runway by the downed Huey we had first seen upon our arrival. We hurriedly gathered up our equipment and headed up the runway to locate the Chinook.

A Chinook helicopter is not an easy piece of equipment to hide even in the jungle so we quickly traced the aircraft just off the concrete run way. For those who don't know, the Chinook helicopter is a metal tube with two large whirling horizontal blades projecting from each end. The forward end is the pilot's cockpit while the back end has two motors and a loading ramp. Of course they are painted olive drab with olive drab trim just for uniformity.

The CH-47 Chinook is a mighty cargo type of helicopter that can sling heavy loads like artillery pieces under its fuselage or load a jeep and trailer inside by driving up the rear ramp. The CH-47 is a large vibrating, bellowing, lumbering beast that has often saved the day for American soldiers around the world. So with great hopes of saving our day, I approached the crew chief who was standing beside the lowered rear ramp. He was wearing a flight helmet that contained a microphone and headset with a long cord that was plugged into the body of the helicopter and was engaged it a lengthy conversation with, I assumed, the pilot.

When I began to speak the aircrafts rear engines drowned out my words and the crew chief waved us back to a safe spot while continuing his conversation. Realizing I did not know what was going on and that our chances for a ride looked very dismal, I began to scan the area for any other possibilities. Then suddenly the crew chief beckoned me close and asked what I wanted. I yelled my explanation out that we needed to return to Long Binh as soon as possible and hoped to bum a ride anywhere to

THE 3RD HERD – Explosive Ordnance Disposal

the north of Can Tho. He reported what I had said into his microphone then shook his head 'no' as if someone on the other end was making the decision.

"It's against regulation to haul any personnel other than the crew," the crew chief stated flatly. Now, I have seen these behemoths belch out whole vehicles and a squad of men, so what regulation prevented us from riding along, I wondered? I had turned to walk away when the crew chief grabbed me and said to stand over there, pointing to the other side of the loading ramp.

"Be ready to go when I give the word and don't be slow. You are riding at your own risk," he said plainly. I nodded my head before replying, "we've been operating at our own risk ever since we got in-country, this wouldn't be any exception."

With that said he nodded his head, smiled and took his place beside the loading ramp. Finally with everything ready the crew chief yelled go and the three of us scurried up the loading ramp only to find the cargo bay of the helicopter completely empty. We quickly found seats along the perimeter of the cargo bay as the Chinook roared into the sky. The three of us were still at a loss as to what was happening, especially when we realized the helicopter had stopped climbing and was hoovering a few feet off the ground. We watched as the crew chief hurried to the center of the cargo bay floor where he removed a large metal plug before laying down with his head hanging down through the hole.

After a few minutes of this hoovering the huge engines revved up and we began to climb once more with the crew chief still looking down through the hole in the floor. Finally he looked up and waved us to join him on the floor. Peering cautiously through the hole we could see that same broken Huey helicopter hanging directly below on heavy straps known as slings. The aerodynamics of the Huey made it track straight and true but it did swing front to rear in a pendulum fashion. It was a great picture, the smaller Huey gliding along high above the Viet Nam jungle on what was probably its last flight to a salvage yard.

The interior of the Chinook was hot and noisy, the roar and vibration could not be ignored but I noticed the two door gunners, each one facing a square hole on either side of the fuselage were sound asleep. Typical GI's, they had learned the art of catching some zzz's whenever the opportunity arose. Thank you to the crew of this Chinook and so many other flight crews who disobeyed regulations in order to place us in the right place to do our job and return us safely to our unit.

SKY CRANE HEIST

I have often mentioned that a great deal of midnight requisitioning transpired in Viet Nam, possibly to the point that no one believes me anymore. However just to prove my point I will relate a true tale of how material can be redistributed in the military.

It was late evening and the sun was setting in the north once more at Long Binh depot, while S.F.C. Robert Smith had taken up his favorite spot for late evening entertainment. Smitty enjoyed turning on the jeep radios, each one tuned in to a different radio network. This allowed him to eavesdrop on local happenings. One radio carried the calls from Bein Hoa artillery, another dealt with communications from the helicopter units, while a third one carried military police dispatches. This, along with throwing darts at mouse sized cockroaches or provoking a war between the big black ants and the tiny red ant colony constituted our regular evening's entertainment. What an exciting life, the U.S. Army provided everything to keep their well-rounded soldiers well rounded.

In the one year I spent in-country I never saw a movie or a USO show, except the Bob Hope Show which more than made up for missing the other touring shows. The Armed Forces Radio carried an occasional 1930's western while I am sure the weather forecast was a recording. Hot and sunny today, possible rain, warm this evening. Repeat.

Anyway this particular evening Smitty began to call excitedly for us to gather around, we all thought he had overheard something on one of the jeep radios, instead he was pointing to an area just outside our battalion area. Our building was the last one in a row of hooches that any self-respecting hog would refuse to live in. The whole area was a rubber tree grove but we had an open space to our north that allowed us a good view of the happenings in that direction.

As we gathered around, Smitty was pointing past the opening while he kept saying "watch this, watch this." We knew the general area to the north contained a Property Disposal Yard, which is a military version of a civilian junk yard, where old and wrecked vehicles were parted out as needed by motor pools and maintenance units. We knew this PDO yard first hand and since it was within walking distance, our team had made many midnight requisitions from its rows of available parts.

It was only after Smitty pointed out a very

large CH-54 Sky Crane helicopter circling off into the sunset that we all realized something was afoot. Smitty explained he had watched the huge Sky Crane which resembles a gigantic dragon fly approach the PDO yard from the south east. It paused to hover only long enough for two men to repel down a couple of long ropes, then resumed its normal flight pattern. Smitty confidently prophesied the Sky Crane would return shortly and sure enough it could be seen in the dim light of the setting sun heading our way once again. Once the big bird was in position over the PDO yard a cable with a big hook was lowered down to the men on the ground.

"They're going to take something," Smitty calmly decreed and sure enough a damaged Huey helicopter slowly and magically rose above the building and tree tops as if suspended by some nearly invisible thread. We could see the two men who had earlier repelled down the ropes now sitting on the metal deck of the Huey with their legs hung out the open side door. We yelled and waved and they responded in kind, obviously pleased with their evenings work. We watched as the big Sky Crane headed out across Long Binh depot's expansive complex, finally disappearing into the twilight of another perfect Viet Nam night. Needless to say our unit never reported this activity and as far as we ever learned, no action was ever taken in the theft of a multimillion dollar Huey helicopter.

FRIENDLY FIRE

I'm not sure if the incident involving the rocket fired into the conex box full of explosives would be considered friendly fire by those celebrities who without any experience or first-hand knowledge have paid such lip service to these unfortunate events. However I think this example will define just how such tragedies happen.

Once again it was evening and S.F.C. Smith, "Smitty" as we called him, was seated just outside our hooch door monitoring the traffic on our jeep radios when he gave out a call for us to gather around and listen. It seems Bein Hoa Air Base, located just a few miles away had sustained heavy damage to a barracks from three explosions. The radio reported heavy damage and calls were going out for emergency help. It was of course, assumed the projectiles were of Viet Cong origin. While this in itself was not unusual, having three enemy rounds strike such a small target was out of the ordinary.

Smitty called for three men with

equipment to grab a jeep and head to Bein Hoa by the highway that ran out through the open country rather than driving through the streets of the town of Tan Hep. This was bending the rules a bit because we had not been officially notified to respond. He warned the team to keep their radio net clear just in case he needed to contact them in an emergency. I of course volunteered but I had already been scheduled for an early morning helicopter flight so I was barred from making the run. While disappointed at being left behind, all the members present scurried around loading equipment to reduce the team's response time.

With red lights flashing and sirens screaming in order to warn the security people to have the gates open before the team's arrival, our men raced out of the 3rd Ord battalion. Once they cleared Long Binh's main gate they were on their own. With no security forces or MP vehicles to protect them in case of an ambush, they sped on through the darkness.

We stood close to the jeeps hoping to glean more information from their staticy radios while speculating on what had taken place. Some thought it might signal a new Viet Cong offensive, while others believed the attack, due to its proximity to the perimeter wire and three closely spaced detonations, to be the work of sappers. It was at this point that a new report flashed across the air waves indicating three more detonations had occurred in the same barracks. This time not only were the soldiers who lived in the barracks victims, but also the rescue workers, emergency personnel, MP's and just plain GI's who selflessly raced to aid their comrades became the targets of a high explosive detonation.

The call went out for everyone involved in the rescue operation to pull back to a point of safety, whatever that might be. Smitty immediately radioed our team to stop where they were and wait for further instructions. The team replied they had just reached the gate at Bein Hoa Air Base which lay very near the now destroyed barracks. Now the nerve wracking waiting game began, no one could predict if any more explosions would take place but they did know there were wounded and dying men trapped in the partially destroyed building who were in dire need of assistance.

Suddenly before the rescuers could move in again three more explosions ripped through the barracks area stunning everyone concerned. This was not the common Viet Cong attack in the III or IV Corp area because they lacked artillery pieces which used sophisticated sighting devices that could make such accuracy possible. All the attacks we had knowledge of came in the form of mortars, theirs like the 60, 82, and 120 mm. or ours which the VC stole or captured like the 60, 81, and 4.2 inch mortars.

They also employed Chinese 107 mm and 122mm rockets, normally against our larger installation. The rockets were normally fired from improvised launchers using some type of crude homemade delayed timing device. The launchers were nothing more than two boards nailed together in a V formation, or the rocket would rest in the crotch of a tree pointing in our general direction. Other launching devices were merely a mound of dirt and were aimed in a shotgun effect with a great deal of Kentucky windage. So it seemed nearly impossible for Charlie to land nine rounds of explosives in such a small target area.

Finally after much delay and a good deal of caution the emergency personnel reentered the area to begin a long night of morbid rescue and recovery operation. Our team members willingly assisted in any way they could until advised to return to quarters or wherever they deem proper.

It was very late by the time our men negotiated the Viet Cong infested streets and roads that lay between the two large military bases. We flooded them with questions and they did their best to truthfully and respectfully replay the night's activities. I don't recall the death toll or how many men were wounded but I do remember the next morning receiving an official report of the incident.

It was finally discovered that a South Vietnamese l05 mm Artillery Unit had responded to a fire support call at a given map coordinance and they responded by firing three rounds of high explosives on the target. Three more rounds were requested and then three more before it was discovered that somewhere in the operation the coordinance had been reversed 180 degrees. This might have been the fault of the forward observer, or the radio operators, or anyone in between but because of a mistake several good men died and many others were wounded. This is a shining example of friendly fire at its worst.

Carol Burnett made a heart rending movie condemning friendly fire, that I am sure broke many hearts and ripped open the wounds of families and friends of men who had been victims of friendly fire. The term should not be considered detrimental to those who fell victim to its wrath. Friendly fire has gone on since man first made war on other men, it has been present in nearly every armed conflict, be it a declared war, guerilla war, a large or small conflict. Viet Nam was no different than any other war.

Needless to say the Carol Burnett show and any other form of her entertainment is and will always be banned in my household, no question, no argument.

BOB HOPE USO SHOW

Slowly but steadily the scuttlebutt began to spread through the GI's that the Bob Hope Show would play Long Binh this year. We were always hearing rumors such as Red China was going to enter the war and that our unit would be placed under Thai Military Command. One of the more popular rumors had it that the Paris Peace Accord had been signed and everyone would be going home, fill in any date here, of course we all knew that was wishful thinking. The one I wanted to believe came from our own mess Sergeant who claimed that the Army had run out of hot dogs and that they would no longer be served three meals a day. Deep down in my heart I knew this was also wishful thinking because the Army never runs out of hot dogs and even if they did the replacement would be Spam or powdered eggs. So you see it was difficult to believe the rumor mills about the Bob Hope Show coming to Long Binh Post, South Viet Nam.

However our unit began to get conformation that the show would play in our area because the 3rd Herd would be detailed as part of the security force needed to protect the entertainers. As usual, some fly by the seat of your pants plans were made, still very little in the way of firm information was released, possibly for security reasons. Of course everything that happened or didn't happen was for security reasons.

Finally the official word came down that Bob Hope and the Christmas Show would play the amphitheater, a facility I was not sure even existed but I was determine to find its location. Entertainment was scarce in-country and I had been deprived of attending any shows that did make the rounds, so I assumed once again I would be the one to pull duty or go on some long lost bomb call.

We knew the date and time when the show was to take place, only no one had been assigned to be part of the security team. The time was running out for us to appear when it was decided the First Sgt. and a couple of the other upper NCO's would stand by at the building, which in effect allowed the remainder of the lower ranking men to go to the show and pretend to be protecting the celebrities on stage.

I was shocked, and for those of you who don't know RHIP (rank has its privileges) means this should have been a prime example where those with the stripes get the prize details while those with no or lower rank get to do the work. I know for a fact the NCO's who so graciously passed up the afternoon's entertainment wanted to go just as badly as the rest of us but they displayed the mark of good leadership and willingly sacrificed their enjoyment for us. I thank you one and all for the treat of spending a few hours away from the insanity of that war.

Strict orders were given to look presentable and to act in a military manner. We rushed around finding our cleanest fatigues, caps and shined boots, we also had a number of official looking arm bands made of shiny Patton leather with EOD and a bomb sewn in bright colors that we thought would help our little group get closer to the stage.

As we loaded into our vehicles we were once more admonished to perform as professionals, put on a good act and do whatever was required to protect the Hope troop. I'm not sure everyone heard that message but all of us were on our best behavior. We looked like soldiers, acted like soldiers, and performed in a polite non-EOD manner in front of the civilians and especially the many women performers, just the way our leaders wanted us to be.

We arrived at the amphitheater just in time to begin our duties, which was to always make believe we knew what we were doing in any situation which made those not in the know more relaxed and secure. Looking busy and wearing a calm smile went a long way towards unwinding the nerves of the civilians who knew they were in a combat zone and should have been a prized target to the Viet Cong.

I was lucky enough to go back stage where the entertainers were scurrying about making last minute costume adjustments and trying to remain calm. I went into my little dog and pony show checking for explosives and booby traps under and around the stage area which was an open air affair with a big sun shade to shelter the fair skin of those preforming.

I noticed that Bob Hope was staring at me for no apparent reason so I moved on and he did the same, then a few minutes later I caught him looking at me again and believe me I'm not good looking. But I quickly reasoned out that I had spent the day working with Mr. Hope in Ohio where we were pretending to be Secret Service Agents protecting the 1968 presidential candidates. This little charade was against federal law and I didn't desire to lie to Mr. Hope if the subject should come up, so I quickly slipped outside and sent one of the other men in to take my place. This was probably my imagination, but in this case I'd rather be safe than sorry.

When the show got underway a few of our men remained on the wings of the stage while the rest of us found a place on the ground directly in front of the stage. The great nurses from the Medivac Hospital had moved some of their wounded directly in front of the stage between us and the show, but no one complained fearing that to do so might work some kind of karma or bad juju power on us and we would end up wounded in the Medivac Hospital ourselves. Being wounded might have been an early ticket home, but I was willing to do the time if only I could go home with only the holes in my body that the Good Lord had put there.

In fact the heat of the afternoon and the length of the show began to overcome the wounded causing a short interruption until the medical staff could evacuate the affected patients.

The amphitheater was shaped like a bowl with one end removed, everyone sat on the ground, true to the Army way. There were no padded or reclining seats or optima seats except for the communications men who, using their spikes and climbing belts, quickly found perches on top of the several tall light posts.

This drew to the microphone one officer after another, each of a higher rank to order the men to relinquish their towering seats. But with each order the men became more determined to keep their box seats atop the high poles.

Finally in desperation, Mr. Hope moved to the microphone and everyone expected that he would ask in a fatherly voice that the poles be evacuated, instead he asked, "can you climbers see from those lofty positions?"

They quickly acknowledged the view was perfect from that height. Then Mr. Hope asked, "can you remain on those belts and climbers for as long as four hours in this heat?"

Again the men responded positively, to which Mr. Hope replied, "all right then, stay up there."

The crowd roared its approval as the star of the show had just countermanded several officers who were used to being obeyed. True to their word, the pole climbers remained in what I'm sure was their normal work position throughout the entire performance.

Les Brown and his Band of Renown played several songs while the crew moved sets and adjusted electronics. The heat continued to build as only the tropical sun can when you are sitting out in the open. Finally Mr. Hope appeared in an OD green jungle shirt festooned with badges and metals, wearing a cap and wielding his trade mark golf club. Of course he got a standing ovation from the GI's. The man was always savvy enough to have jokes tailored to fit the locals, like officer's names, famous chippy bars, as well as those dealing with any local newsworthy happening. The men loved to hear him make fun of the officers and especially to poke fun at the high ranking officers. But it was all taken good naturedly. In fact, some of those who were the butt of his jokes considered it a mark of distinction indicating they had made it to the top.

I can't remember the order nor all the performers who appeared but Teresa Graves from Laugh In wore a blue thin pants and shirt outfit while dancing a fast paced number that drew a loud applause form the GI's. The very pretty and petit Miss World, sorry I can't remember her name performed several song and dance numbers with Mr. Hope. Connie Stevens was a big hit in her short bright red dress that the men loved. She sang several songs and flirted with all the men. If the heat was bothering her the wide smile on her face and her fast movements around the edge of the stage covered the fact completely.

She asked for volunteers named Bill to come up on the stage. Ten or twelve men responded and of course when she asked each individual his name it came out that a couple of the men were not really named Bill. She laughed and joked while she sang the song "Bill" to these lucky and elated group of would-be Williams. To say the woman was a sensation that was talked about for days after the show is an understatement. In fact, I just recently heard a man recalling Miss Stevens' performance that day.

As a surprise guest, Mr. Hope led Neil Armstrong, attired in his NASA jumpsuit out on the stage. Mr. Armstrong had just days before been the first man to walk on the moon and twenty five thousand GI's gave the man a long standing ovation. We were close enough to see the startled and shy look on the man's face. He moved to the microphone but was too flabbergasted to talk in a normal manner. Out of that mass of men I knew there was a large number who had faced injury and death many times in the last year, I for one felt proud of the men present that day for giving this true American hero the out pouring of respect and admiration that he deserved.

One of the true highlights of the show was the Gold Diggers, a song and dancers troop who were regulars on the very successful Dean Martin television show that was so popular back in the world. The group consisted of a dozen beautiful young ladies who performed perfectly in the unbearable heat, they gave their heart and soul to bring some joy to the lonely soldiers in the audience. Those home in the world can never appreciate the gift of seeing a beautiful round eyed girl even from a distance.

Mr. Hope knew his craft well and supplied a stage full of beautiful dignified ladies. There wasn't any off-colored humor nor profanity, only good natured fun and good music and a lot of laughs. We all respected each and every man and woman who took the stage that unmercifully hot afternoon in a jungle that now seems too far away.

I know that every man and woman who witnessed one of the many Bob Hope Shows, whether it was WW II, Korea or Viet Nam will always remember and be eternally grateful to Mr. Hope and the cast and crew who gave so much of themselves to become what was the highlight of their in-country tour to many.

Thank you Mr. Hope and all of those people who made these mini R&R's so enjoyable. I know there were twenty five thousand men who exited that make-shift amphitheater on that hot afternoon who were walking on air and wearing a smile from ear to ear.

ROAD CLOSED

Another illustration of how easy it is to become cannon fodder in that or any war I will tell you of an act of complete stupidity on my part that could have easily ended differently.

My partner, Walter Gee and I received an urgent call for help from a small base outside of the Long Binh bunker line. We both knew the different roads to that base and made a rapid decision as to the best and fastest possible route to be taken. We were driving hard, passing everything on the small back trails, sliding corners while hitting the siren and yelling at the locals to get out of our way. We powered the jeep around a ninety degree corner that took us off the main road and into a large field that had been cleared down to the dirt.

We slowed down long enough to read the big official painted sign that warned the road was closed but there wasn't any indication as to why the road was closed. We could see that after clearing, the road bed had been rebuilt above the surrounding field. It seemed reasonable to us the closed road was in all actuality still open. Besides we were in a hurry to respond to the emergency call so when my partner who was driving asked what we should do I said, "floor it" and he did.

The little jeep picked up speed and about half way across the opening and not very far ahead of us all hell broke loose as several 40mm high explosive rounds cut a swath from the north side of the road to the south side. My partner slid the little jeep to a stop and calmly stated, "duster compound," as if it was a daily occurrence being shelled by these deadly projectiles.

There was in fact, a duster compound just to the north of this empty field, so we speculated as we waited for the dust to clear that the barren field was used to test their weapons, or to sight in the twin barreled guns or possibly an open field of fire if they were attacked by Viet Cong troops.

The weapon known as the M42 duster in Viet Nam was composed of two 40mm guns that were mounted atop a self-propelled track vehicle. The guns are fed by clips that hold four rounds of high explosives, possibly self-destructing artillery shells that are fed and ejected automatically.

After the dust cleared and we realized no damage had been done, my partner posed the question of what we should do next. I looked all around for any indication of what to expect next before saying "let's go." Now I want it known that my partners, whoever they might be, had just as much say-so in these situations but by remaining silent they were agreeing to my decisions. We peeled out frantically shifting gears and picking up speed until reaching the opposite side of the open field.

We had other occasions to make calls on that particular duster compound and each time I would bring up the subject of those high explosive shells impacting just in front of our jeep but I never got any explanation as to why it happened. I have often wondered if some clown fired just in front of us to make a point that the road was closed. Still if they had errored in aiming we could have been listed with those reported as killed by friendly fire.

Walter Gee, Wheel Man

MILITARY ISSUE

By the time I reached Viet Nam, I came to the conclusion the EOD units were considered the poor ugly stepchild of the Army when it came to being issued anything. It was bad enough back in the states but because of short supply, requesting nearly any item from the supply system in-country was a complete exercise in futility. Simple things like uniforms and boots let alone weapons or radios would be met with a blank stare from the issuing office.

My first weapon in-country was a Thomson submachine gun and a bag full of ammo that weighed nearly as much as I did which was about two hundred and thirty pounds at the time. Carrying that weapon and a forty pound bag of C-4 around made me fearful of being near any body of water. I was a strong swimmer but I quickly come to realize that falling into the Mekong River or any of its many tributaries would result in guaranteed drowning.

We obtained most of our jungle

fatigues, boots, canteens, and web gear from the Medivac Hospitals when responding to their calls for help with hand grenades, claymore mines, C-4 and other explosives items that were removed from the dead and wounded soldiers clothing and field packs.

On arriving at the Medivac Hospital the soldiers were stripped of their muddy and bloody gear in preparation for treatment. Those items were cleaned and placed in their store room to be reissued if that patient were sent back to the field or shipped back home. Much of this equipment was never reissued so we bummed what we could from the hospital supply Sergeants.

The newly issued jungle fatigues, if obtainable, were dyed a funny green and had a stiff shiny finish that marked you as a newbie to other GI's but even worse to the local Vietnamese population. The local merchants and general population who, upon seeing these new uniforms, would try to take advantage of the new soldiers in-country. Being small, close knit units, we would normally explain the bright green shiny uniforms to the new men in-country and quickly outfit them with old faded fatigues. However some men were superstitious about wearing or using equipment once belonging to a dead man which is foolish because many items are recovered from the dead and wounded and are reissued through proper military supply chains. If you think Uncle Sam retires the weapons from every soldier who dies in combat, the Army would quickly have a shortage of usable weapons. My partners and I had no such qualms about the dead, we handled their bodies regularly, had to wash their blood and body fluids from our skin and clothing and even went so far as to eat their rations when we became hungry. It was, after all, a war where you accept in order to survive. We never dishonored the dead American soldiers or the dead Viet Cong either, feeling that they were loyal and brave members of their organizations, and were quite willing to allow us to take their lives. It's hard not to have some respect for people who are willing to make that sacrifice.

The old time soldiers used to say "you can't steal in the Army only from it," meaning if the stolen item was to be used for military purposes it was all right, but if you stole Army goods for sale or trade on the black market you were wrong. That saying became the motto of many EOD men after following proper procedure failed to provide needed supplies. However, occasionally we stretched this saying to the breaking point.

As an example, as I mentioned my first weapon was a Thompson Submachine gun, that was followed by an old M1 thirty caliber carbine, then by a battered M14, none of which had come through the unit armorer. Finally I was legally issued a decent M14 rifle, which did function most of the time, one you could feel relatively safe carrying outside of a parade ground.

Many people would say this was no big deal and aside from trying to protect yourself it was important because every soldier is issued two weapons cards that show the model and serial number of your issued firearm. Understand if you are stopped by the MP's and your weapons card doesn't match your weapons serial number or if it's not the type or number that the unit armorer has on file or if you are involved in a questionable shooting either with our personnel or theirs, your life can turn around in short order.

A person needed to be aware of what was in their procession at all times but we seldom did. For instance, if you had been issued or loaned a weapon that had been used in a crime and were caught with it, needless to say a great deal of explaining would be required and even that might not be enough to save you.

We had soldiers and civilians approach us from time to time with a request that we blow up a particular weapon to prevent its rifling being examined. The reason for this should be obvious, these weapons had been involved in some type of crime. I would refuse to answer any questions on that subject but such things did take place. Weapons were indeed destroyed for various reasons, the number one reason was that a projectile had not cleared the gun barrel and had become stuck in the rifling. The weapons in question either carried paper work for their disposal or it was a field expedient to prevent such firearms from falling into the enemies hands or into those of criminals within the military ranks.

The use of high explosives on weapons including M-16 up to large artillery pieces was always an enjoyable assignment. One of our favorites involved the use of explosives to dislodge an artillery projectile from the large gun's tube. The 155mm, 175mm guns seemed, at least to me, more prone to such failures. I'm sure other ordnance people would name different weapons as troublesome.

We did respond to calls from mortar crews who claimed their 60 or 81mm mortar had a projectile lodged in its tube. These situations involved nothing more than inverting the smooth mortar tube to allow the projectile to slide out. It may sound funny but some mortar crews either did not know of this procedure or they were afraid to attempt such a maneuver.

Many of these weapon failures were caused by poor maintenance by the individual soldier or his issuing armorer and many times we discovered upon responding to calls that neglect or irresponsible handling was the culprit. One such incident centered on a very remote Thai artillery base. My partner and I had been told to rush to the Medivac Hospital as a Huey was waiting to transport us into the middle of nowhere.

Upon arriving at the Thai fire base we found several 105mm Howitzers that had been burned or blown up. Most of the buildings and bunkers in the compound showed signs of blasts and fire. The area was littered with propellant charges as well as propellant cans, black powder bags, 105mm and 155mm high explosives and white phosphorus artillery shells.

Some of these projectiles were fused while others had round lifting rings in the fuse wells. The partially buried bunkers were flattened and had been on fire or blown apart. It was obvious that some sort of devastation had hit the base but it was unlike anything we had seen before which peaked our curiosity.

The Thai soldiers, officers and enlisted merely smiled and bowed politely when questioned about what had transpired.

"Was it a rocket or mortar attack, or had VC sappers infiltrated the camp?" we asked without any positive response. Then finally one officer came forward and stated the men were having a celebration the night before and as the merriment increased, the gunners began to fire propellant charges less the projectiles into the air. After some more fun, the gunners began to lower the gun barrels so they could fire down the main street of the base. The flames from the propellant charges set fire to some of the bunker material and the fire spread unabated until its heat began to set off high explosive rounds. Needless to say, the area was in sad repair but no one seemed to take the matter seriously. Just something that might happen to a bunch of boys playing with fire.

The cleanup was a daunting task as some hazardous devices were buried under piles of dirt and rubble while others were in the bottom of the collapsed bunkers. We were accustom to the problems and hazards pertaining to leaking white phosphorus rounds and hundreds of pounds of black powder, not to mention high explosives scattered about the base but we were not accustom to working with this particular Thai unit. In short order we discovered not only a language barrier but we also suffered from a common sense barrier. As it happened this unit was recruited from members of the Bangkok circus.

The unit was made up of jugglers, kick boxers and acrobats and everyone wanted to show off for us. The Thai soldiers would, without warning and at any second begin to juggle ordnance items that were sensitive to handle, things that were dangerous to move let alone toss around. It was like trying to corral a bunch of first graders only these kids were grown men who didn't understand our warnings and could care less at what the results might be.

A good deal of loose white phosphorus had gotten covered by dark loose dirt which kept the oxygen from igniting the white phosphorus, as long as it remained covered but if touched or stepped on white smoke would begin to rise up through the dirt piles. The magical white smoke wafting up through the black earth was as tempting to these men as candy to a baby. No matter how much we warned them about receiving skin burns the Thais would dive into the dirt digging like a wild dog.

I have to admit I did derive some perverse pleasure from their howling and dancing about after being burned by the white phosphorus.

As it turned out we completed the cleanup with only a few minor moments of terror and the Thai soldiers seemed to enjoy working with us disregarding the injuries they received. They considered the whole affair a humorous lark and after trying to talk to such people it becomes obvious you can't win so you just go with the flow and hope for good luck. The enlisted men ran around performing stupid stunts while the few officers in camp ignored their men's actions.

All in all it was one of those unique experiences that only the military can provide, experiences that are not planned or scripted that can only happen by accident.

I should add that some of the Thai units we worked with were very military, no improv comedy or standup comics but real soldiers who stayed straight and served with honor.

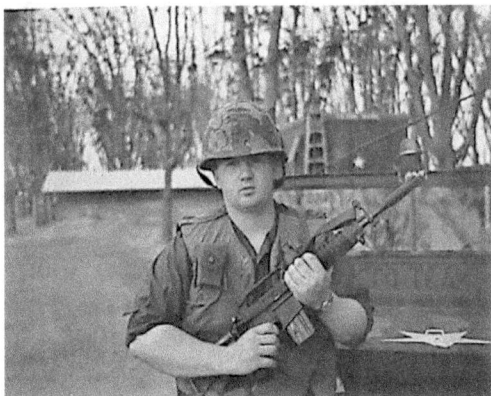

GARY POOL WITH CAR 15

THAI FOOD

Eating with the Thais was always a unique and often times thrilling adventure. I have to laugh at those cooking shows on TV that make a big deal out of dining on unusual or strange delicacy.

My first contact with the Thais and their diets came only days after my arrival in-country. I have no recollection of the incident nor where we went but I do remember getting set back on my heels by an American Major who was half Thai.

At noon a Thai soldier approached me with a very large platter covered with rice and one of the largest Carp or rough fish I had ever seen. I say that with some caution having been raised on the banks of the Missouri River where we ran hoop nets for substance fishing. But this fish was huge and had not been cleaned. Head, scales, guts, and glassy eye balls were quite obvious. One look and I turned the fish and rice down knowing you should never consume raw fish.

Asia and much of the world consider a rejection of any food or drink as a major social insult. It was only moments before the Army Major stomped over to where I was sitting on the ground screaming out orders that I eat this dish. It was after all, he said, a great delicacy that the Thais had gone to a great deal of effort in preparing in my honor. "It would," he said, "cause him to lose face among his own people."

I apologized and ask him to relay my gratitude and explain I was having stomach trouble and would not eat anything that day. But no matter what I said or how earnest I was, he would not accept my attempts to smooth the matter over, the Major just continued to bellow one direct order after another. He made some veiled threats both physical and legal and promised at the least to call my Commanding Officer to have me punished for refusing to follow his direct order.

When I finally had heard enough, I jumped to my feet and faced the man who was attired in field gear. He wore a metal helmet and full web gear, he carried an M-16 and a big dislike for me. I, on the other hand, was dressed in dirty baggy fatigues, jungle hat and little else. I managed to keep my temper while explaining that the Army had warned us because of illness not to eat or drink anything provided by the local citizens. I admit we broke this rule many times but it seemed like a good excuse in this situation. But he was not buying my argument and kept repeating his order that I eat the big ugly Carp, scales, entrails and all.

I have never been an accomplished debater or quick witted so I quickly ran out of points or counter points to present. I quickly realized I had once again come to the edge of the cliff, the precipice, point of no return, either put up or shut up, a point that could change my life and future. I simply explained such an order was not legal, that no one in or out of the military could make me eat or drink anything I did not wish to. Furthermore, I stated flatly that neither he nor his Thai soldiers could make me eat that raw fish.

We parted company then. I completed all the EOD work on the site and found a ride back to Long Binh and the 3rd Ord EOD building. I have to give the Major credit for being true to his word about calling in a report to my Commanding Officer.

On arrival I was met by the First Sgt. who had taken the Majors call and he was, needless to say, a bit irate. After a good scolding, I repeated the same ultimatum that I gave the Major in the field, fully expecting another lecture, the First Sgt. shook his head stating that I was right but that I should be careful about who I challenged in these confrontations. I knew there was a hidden message in what the First Sgt. said and that was, "you can square off against anyone you like except me. Don't ever cross me."

I was never foolish enough to argue with that man because I would lose the fight as many enlisted men and officers learned over the length of their illustrious service career.

I know all this sounds childish and a minor event and yet I have found one of the best ways to quickly get to know a person is challenge them when a questionable decision is made. If they stand true to their actions that man is probably trustworthy. On the other hand if they hedge or back down you'd better beware. Of course with some men, like the First Sgt. I mentioned, no testing was needed; you could be sure his words were the law of the land.

IT'S MY HAMBURGER

A good many people don't fully understand the military's rules and regulation when it comes to respecting rank. But basically the rule is you can't hit anyone, no one superior to your rank, or any one below your rank, or any one in your rank. So why didn't they just say you can't hit anyone, but that wouldn't be the military way.

Going into basic training is like the first day of kindergarten, don't wet your pants, be quiet, play well with others and for God sake never hit another person. I always thought this a very strange rule for an organization that trains its members to kill other people or in some cases kill lots of other people.

Now don't get me wrong, I realize the need for discipline in the military for without control over its members nothing would get done and the place would be a mad house. Still some things are just too good to be true, like the case of a young Spec 4 I served with.

It was just after lunch, another meal the Spec 4 and I had gladly missed at the mess hall. The EOD building was nearly empty except for our First Sgt. and his best friend, an E-6 from an EOD unit up north. They were sitting in our dayroom/bar when the telephone rang so I took the call.

The Spec 4 said he was going to the trash truck, hoagie bait truck, or whatever derogatory name you can come up with to describe it because this vehicle was definitely not a snack bar or lunch wagon. He asked if I wanted anything but I wisely declined and I continued taking the phone call. In just seconds the Spec 4 had returned with two hamburgers and seemed well satisfied with the score while signaling he was going into our dayroom to eat.

The EOD building's office door sat just adjoining the door to the dayroom and I saw my friend open the door and enter but just as quickly he came running back out the door yelling something I didn't understand. I interrupted the call long enough to find out that our First Sergeant's best friend had, without so much as a by your leave, grabbed one of the two hamburgers and took a big bite of it.

The Spec 4 was understandably irate at the Staff Sergeant's improper etiquette and demanded I do something about it. I explained I was taking a bomb call and that it wasn't my hamburger because if it was, I would have already knocked the E-6 on his butt.

I went back to the phone call thinking the matter settled when suddenly the air was filled with yelling and profanity. I dropped the phone and raced into the day room to find the Spec 4 standing at attention while the Staff Sergeant and our First Sgt. were busy screaming threats at the top of their lungs.

I realized the Spec 4 had taken my words to heart and had indeed punched the Staff Sergeant in the mouth for taking a bite out of his hamburger. As usual this instantly became my fault as the Spec 4 reported that I had told him to strike the E-6 and the two higher ranking Sergeants immediately turned their combined wrath on me. When they demanded to know if I had told the young man to hit the Staff Sergeant I figured there was no point arguing and said I had so instructed him, adding if it had been my hamburger I would have broken the Sergeant's jaw.

As you can imagine several long hot minutes passed as we three threatened each other while the E-4 stood silently at attention. I heard physical threats, court martial threats, a promise of losing my stripes, or being transferred to some other unit.

It was at that very moment I knew all would turn out well, because I knew no other unit would accept me. As for losing my rank, I knew I could resign from EOD at any time and go back into ammunition storage, my first MOS but rank meant little to me as most of us were already filling a rank above which was against regulations. The physical threats were easy of ignore, both men would be a worthy opponent in a bar room brawl but that would place them on par with the Spec 4.

The offer of a court martial always made me a little nervous each and every time I was offered such punishment but even that concerned me only because my parents had warned me if I were to get court martialed and especially if I got a dishonorable discharge there was no coming home. In the case of a dishonorable discharge, my parents made it clear that I should "never darken their doorway, just keep moving," they would say in no uncertain terms.

I always thought it strange in all these little differences no one ever offered to kick me out of EOD, losing my badge was the only thing I really feared during these little scrapes.

The yelling continued which was fine with me, but in the end I told the Staff Sergeant that he was in our building as a guest and he should conduct himself accordingly. He was way out of line taking advantage of one of our team members and fellow EOD men.

I then told them they could do their damndests to punish me but at the moment I was in the middle of a bomb call and that's the reason I came to Viet Nam. I walked out of the dayroom, signaling the Spec 4 to follow just to get him out of more trouble.

I managed to contact the person who had reported the bomb call and told him I would be to his location in just a moment. I told the Spec 4 to grab his gear as we were going on a call, then I relayed the information to the two Sergeants who were still in the dayroom red faced and fuming over what had taken place.

The Spec 4 and I were lucky as the call took up most of the afternoon, it would have taken even longer but I ran out of stalling tactics. We rolled back in to our area about sunset and went about business as usual. Nothing was ever said about the fracas or who did or said what. All the members of our little unit returned safely home that evening and quickly bellied up to the bar in our dayroom. All was forgiven, an EOD team was saved that night over a cold beer, the elixir that was the answer to all and any problems, be they personal, or military.

I never drank while in-country but many a night I was glad to buy another round in order to promote peace and harmony among the troops. Maybe some of our political leaders should give good old beer a chance when they are in negotiations with our adversaries.

THE BOLDEST EOD MAN

All right, I confess, I have told this story many times before and it has been in print but I must recount it here to honor a brave man. People don't believe this tale but I swear it is the honest truth. Better yet, I can if need be, get others who were present to vouch for what transpired.

Our day room was no more than a square windowless box, the west wall held the back door and a padded bar with its line of refrigerators just behind. The west wall and door were opposite the east door that led into our building proper. Four or five small tables were scattered about the floor still allowing easy movement for table hopping. But there among the tables and out of place sat a cheap plastic chaise lounge that occupied a great deal of space when unfolded and it was always unfolded.

This fugitive from a junk yard constituted the first rule of operation I was given on the first day I arrived at the 3rd Ord EOD. "Never ever sit in the chaise lounge," I was warned repeatedly.

It was unquestionably the sole property of the First Sergeant and our Top Sergeant was a soldier no one wanted to offend.

The second set of instructions I got covered the rules of disturbing the First Sgt. when he was napping in his chair, that being you could politely approach him only in a soft voice IF and only IF the massive Long Binh ammunition depot had blown up. This ruling of the chaise lounge was quickly passed along to any stranger who happened to visit our bar. The really strange thing to me was observing visitors' reactions to this rule and they were all the same. Some of these men were high ranking officers, some were important soldiers from allied countries, some were pretty tough men who liked to challenge any such edict but each and every one smiled and nodded to indicate they would willingly comply with the rules of the house.

Time passed and I got to know the First Sgt. fairly well, he was the kind of man everyone respected; loved and respected or hated and respected but they did show respect in his presence. I must add at this point that our Top Sgt. was something of a legend in the EOD community, a man who after thirty odd years in the military had done it all from WWII, to Korea, and now Viet Nam. By this time the man attended few bomb calls but I was fortunate enough to be selected to partner with him on a couple of good calls. I can truthfully say the Top Sgt. and I never became good friends or even friends for that matter, but he was a man of great poise who kept his calm demeanor even when working on a particularly ticklish piece of ordnance. Respect is the only word in the dictionary to define this man.

One day we were notified that an old minefield had been discovered outside of Vung Tau, and it would have to be cleared. Both Vung Tau which was an in-country R&R destination and the minefield lay within the 3rd Ord EOD area of responsibility. The word came down that our team would be given the assignment of several days' work clearing and disarming these mines.

The team was quietly excited at being given such an opportunity. I had never been closer than the outskirts of Vung Tau and was hopeful of being selected for the team. Hopeful, that is until the Top Sgt. said "no, clearing mine fields qualified as engineers work" and we would not be clearing that minefield or any other as long as he remained First Sgt. Naturally everyone voiced their disappointment including a young Captain who was our Commanding Officer but it was to no avail. The team members accepted the unhappy decree and went about our business for we all knew no one could change the Top Sergeant's mind once he had made a decision.

The matter had all but been forgotten until a few days later as I walked into the bar with a sandwich from the trash truck. It was my favorite sub, the one with shiny slick green cold meat on a soggy bun.

Just as I took a seat the First Sgt. walked in and sat down on his private chaise lounge, leaned back and got comfortable before covering his face with his Army issue baseball cap. Several team members were at different tables but the one I occupied was right next to the prized chaise lounge.

Shortly the door from our office opened and in stepped our Commanding Officer accompanied by a Major of unknown origin, which in itself was not unusual for many, many strangers passed through the 3rd Ord door. However, I could see by the look on our Captain's face and his action this would be a different type of meeting. Our Captain nervously introduced the Major to our Top Sgt. who never made a move or responded to the officer's presence, he just lay still with his cap covering his face.

Our Captain stammered through the reason for the Major's visit and that was to induce our team to proceed to Vung Tau to clean up the abandoned minefield. It was explained that the mines in this location were M-14 or as we called them shoe mines. The mines were small and round, made of mostly plastic which prevented the use of mine detectors, but it was promised overlay maps would be provided. Overlay maps are useful but these small mines had a habit of moving when buried in sandy soil especially for a long period of time as these had been.

The Major was obviously doing a slow burn but really flew mad after the First Sgt. merely responded with a strong "no" through the his hat.

Now remember the two officers were on their feet while our Top Sgt. remained reclined in his chaise lounge, hat covering his face. For some reason this Major refused to accept the Tops firm "no," and anyone with the slightest bit of people-skills would have sensed that when this old Sergeant said "no" he meant "NO!"

The Major then asked the young CO, "who runs this unit, you or this Sergeant?" The thought raced through my mind, I think we have already settled that point Major. I inhaled a deep breath, fearing what was to happen next and it did.

The CO wisely replied that the Top Sgt. did indeed make such decisions. The Major made one more attempt to bully the two men into doing his will but once again the old man under the cap answered an emphatic "NO." The Major, finally realizing he was not going to get his way, flew into a rage.

"Sergeant!" the Major bellowed, "when you speak to me you will rise to your feet and address me as Sir!"

"F--- you Major," the Top Sgt. replied in a loud clear voice without rising from his chaise lounge or removing his cap from his face. The young CO, normally ruddy faced, became a pasty white as he struggled to say the right thing to smooth over the situation.

I fully expected the offended Major to order us to bring our First Sgt. to his feet, but that would have only produced a mutiny. I'm not sure which team members were present in our bar that day but I can state positively, not a man among us would have lifted a hand against the Top Sgt. and maybe the Major realized that and stopped before he made a fool of himself or to have the situation escalate any further.

The disgruntled Major stomped out of our dayroom with our CO following close behind. I'm not sure what passed between the two officers as they faced off in our outer office, but I do know my brain quickly kicked into passing gear at the thought of being a witness to a court martial. I had been seated only a couple of feet from the famous chaise lounge and could not prevent hearing what took place. My poor underpowered brain began smoking, it was turning so fast. Why you might ask? Because this Top Sgt. was known and admired throughout the EOD community which was a very small community and it would have been unwise to testify against him. It was so small an organization at that time that if you were to testify against this man during a court martial, leaving the field would be your only hope.

I don't mean to air their dirty laundry in public, but leave it to say the field culled its own herd, and there were some very cunning and serious cowboys riding herd on that MOS.

The days passed and nothing was said about the flare up in the bar, still we all waited patiently for the hammer to fall. I couldn't believe that nothing had happened, no court martial, thank God, no written or verbal reprimand, the whole affair was dropped and never mentioned again, well not quite again. I have always been one to stir the pot or inquire when silence should have been golden. A couple of weeks later I was told the Top Sgt. and I were going to helicopter to a mortar platoons distant fire base. The flight was enjoyable as we passed over an area that I had never seen from either the air or the ground.

The call turned out to be nothing more than a nice flight, the ordnance involved the 4.2 inch mortar. We were told the gunners had fired a number of short rounds that had landed inside the parameter wire. We inspected all the 4.2 shell bodies and quickly determined they were not short rounds but expended illumination or flare rounds.

A short artillery round is one that falls short of its intended target, and while still filled with its payload, its fuse may or may not be armed. The illumination rounds were fired into the air where the back end falls off dragging a flare out to light up the night. Once the illumination round has fully functioned, no explosive hazard should be present. Whoever called in this incident did not know ordnance very well or possibly just thought it would be fun to call the EOD.

We reported our findings and gave a short class on illuminating rounds with emphasis on 4.2 mortar rounds. We gathered up some of the expended 4.2 inch steel bodies and pointed out the similarities to unfired H.E. projectiles. The 4.2 inch mortar shells being spin stabilized lack the obvious lower fins of the 60, 80, 81, or 120 mm projectiles. The 4.2 inch shells have a round tube attached to its base and this is where the propellant is located. After firing, the fuse blows the baseplate and tube off, allowing a parachute to deploy. Both the tail section and main body drop to the earth leaving a lot of metal in its wake. So you can see it is possible for an uninitiated person looking on from a distance to declare these bodies as short rounds.

This unit was a mortar platoon who

should have been trained in the use of 4.2 inch mortar shells. It was another case of poor training or an officer in charge who should not have been making such decisions.

In any case the First Sgt. and I began to ask around about transportation back to Long Binh and true to form, none was available. Then we were informed that all the helicopters were gone but there was a fixed wing getting ready for takeoff and if we hurried we might catch a ride with him. We hurried to the little air strip in time to see the most miss-begotten aircraft I had ever laid eyes on.

The aircraft was a single engine whose cowling seemed to stretch on forever ending with a huge propeller up front, a long shiny aluminum body with several windows down each side and a large tail that seemed completely out of proportion to the rest of the craft. The First Sergeant, a private pilot, was obviously excited at the thought of being transported in this ungainly looking plane.

The pilot was just warming up for take-off when the First Sgt. opened the side door and asked if we could hitch a lift to anywhere near Long Binh. We were in luck, the plane was headed for Bien Ho Air Base which lay very close to Long Binh and our sister EOD unit, the 42nd was located there so we were automatically assured a meal and if need be a bed for the night.

The plane was an Air America ship that was usually flown by civilians, say the CIA, making the flight back very interesting.

But what I want to relay to the reader is the reply given when I approached the First Sgt. about his swearing at the Major in our dayroom. He calmly answered that he had the private phone numbers of high ranking officers and diplomats all the way from Saigon to the Pentagon, also that he had over 30 years of active duty and had no desire to be in South Viet Nam. The Top Sgt. also stated the Army could send him home at any time as he had requested, but some of these powerful friends had asked him to do them a favor and cover a unit because of the personnel shortage. Always a man of his word, the First Sgt. remained on duty until properly relieved.

Now if you are wondering what happened to the minefield at Vung Tau, which started this lengthy tale? Well, the 42nd EOD called and wanted to know if they could take on the job of clearing the minefield and our First Sgt. was happy to hand off the task to them with a stern warning of the dangers involved. We all had friends in the 42nd and were glad to see them have an assignment in an R&R center but naturally we couldn't help but envy that team until we got the call.

It seems one of the small mines had been

overlooked for whatever reason and their First Sgt. had kneeled down on it causing a detonation that removed his leg at the knee. The blast also struck his partner in the face causing him to lose his sight. A third team member was located at a safe distance. It was his task to disarm the mines and observe the movement of his teammates in case an accident might take place.

The team had a Medic on hand but he refused to enter the minefield to help the wounded soldiers. The man who had been disarming the mines grabbed the stretcher and hurried to his teammates who at this point were helpless. At the blast site, the third man deployed the stretcher before leading the blinded man to a position at one end of the stretcher where he could reach the handles. He then hurried to place the injured First Sgt. on the stretcher and as he said for some unknown reason, he stepped to the side to retrieve the First Sgt. severed leg in order to place it on the stretcher beside the Sergeant. The effort proved tragic as he stepped on another mine which blew off some of his toes, with pieces of the mine traveling up his leg to become imbedded in his groin.

All three men remained calm as the third man took up a positon at the front handles on the stretcher and the blinded soldier at the other end, and with great poise he led all three out of the mine field to safety. It was, to say the least, a valorous act when one man leaves a place of safety to enter a mine field only to be wounded himself before leading his blinded comrade and First Sgt. back to safety.

However the unfortunate incident served to justify our 3rd Ord's First Sgt. when he had flatly refused the Majors demand that he send his men into such a highly dangerous situation when it was likely to end badly as it had for the 42nd team.

CHEMICAL WARFARE

Our team received numerous calls to inspect captured ammunition for any dangerous material or explosive ordnance. These caches might be right on a post or far out in the jungle, in either case our units would respond to all such calls. We all studied the ordnance, curious to see anything new that Charlie might decide to deploy, we would occasionally find old French and Japanese explosive devices. Some of these old weapons were unstable and sensitive to work with. When I say new explosive devices, I mean that South East Asia had been an open marketplace for weapons and gun runners since before WWII and the trade now, although mostly run through Red China, was still open for business.

It was not unusual to find firearms manufactured in Czechoslovakia, Yugoslavia, Poland, or any other Iron Curtain country on the battlefields or in captured caches. We were often warned by the intelligence department to watch for various new items they had reason to believe were coming down the Hoa Chi Mein trail.

At one point in the war, word came down that a Russian Colonel had been killed just south of Saigon. The bad part, he had in his possession a full chemical suit, testing equipment, and antidotes for chemical agents. You hear these stories all the time; a percentage are true, some are half-truths while others are complete lies. This information was direct from the brass and disseminated at a meeting I attended in Saigon's MACV Office. But the inference was that if there were outsiders of any rank with chemical suits there was a distinct possibility that there were chemical weapons in South Viet Nam.

I can confirm the Russian chemical suit and equipment because I saw and touched it in Saigon at the meeting. I can't however confirm where the equipment came from but it was clearly of Soviet manufacture and under comparison, it was easy to determine which items were meant for what tasks. Basically any chemical qualified man in the room could have, with a little thinking, donned the suit and fulfilled a mission.

This disclosure of possible chemical weapons in South Viet Nam presented a lot of problems for those of us who would be called upon to dispose of any such ordnance. One of the first problems encountered was the lack of chemical equipment in-country. As far as we the people who would be called on to dispose of these deadly weapons, had no knowledge of the existence of chemical suits or equipment or where it might be accessed if it did in fact exist.

Knowing the introduction of chemical or biological weapons in South Viet Nam would have been a major escalation in the war, we were told to use extra care when approaching anything unusual, foreign ordnance or while inspecting arms caches.

In the days following the military's disclosure of the possible presence of chemical weapons in-country, our unit received an odd call from a security team in the Delta. As usual two of us were given the assignment and were ready to depart when our First Sgt. decided to join us. His only reason for the change was based on a vague phone call from the security team; that and a little voice that kept telling the First Sgt. something wasn't right. Listening to what the little voices said to bomb disposal teams often played a big role in their actions.

We three loaded up and headed into the Delta, sure of our objective and after a lot of map reading and wrong turns we finally located the security team's compound. Being lost on calls was not unusual, what with the lack of road and street signs at least those printed in English being quite common. However taking the wrong turn down some abandoned dirt road could prove to be a fatal mistake.

The security personnel told a story of being attacked in the early morning hours by a VC unit that had deployed a strange explosive device. The security people pointed out one such device that had failed to function. It could be seen laying on bare open ground about one hundred yards outside of the team's perimeter wire. When asked to accompany us, they flatly refused to give us any support or cover saying that was our responsibility, not theirs. I was shocked at their actions, after all it was their area to defend and protect, the more men in the group the less chance of being attacked.

Irregardless we moved forward with all eyes open and senses alert, fully expecting to encounter trouble. A slow cautious approach brought us near the suspected item which turned out to be a burlap wrapped cube that was tied up in shiny wires like a present. This careful approach was necessary to help detect any hidden mines or booby traps that Charlie was so fond of using as back up on such items. When all appeared clear we started to disarm the device, which was an explosive catapult, its intent is to use one explosive charge to propel another explosive device into the enemy's lines.

The soft soil around the package contained a good deal of sign where Charlie had prepared the explosive before moving off in the direction of a bamboo thicket that lay close enough to be used as cover to attack our team or hide Charlie as he waited to detonate a different explosive device against our team.

I picked up Charlie's trail as the other two team members began to dismantle the burlap wrapped cube. Being able to track and read sign, a skill most of our team members were proficient with, came in very handy when approaching booby traps. The tracks I followed were made by Ho Chi Mien sandals that were famous for being manufactured from the treads of old truck tires.

The soft soil and homemade sandals combined to make tracking very easy, perhaps too easy but I followed what appeared to be three VC into the bamboo thicket. This bamboo was of a large diameter, set close together and very tall. It was so thick that one couldn't see more than a foot in any one direction.

The sandal tracks led toward the middle of the bamboo patch but I couldn't see anyone within the always moving sea of grass. I could however hear movement as more than one individual attempted to slither through the maze undetected.

Charlie's sandal tracks were quite visible in the soil of the bamboo thicket but were very difficult to follow unless you moved to a point nearly on top of the tracks. I moved with all stealth through the bamboo wanting to know where these three VC might go and what they were up to.

I feared they would circle back through the bamboo and ambush my teammates whose attention was directed to disarming the explosives on the burlap wrapped package. Or even worse, they might remotely function a third explosive charge or Claymore mine directed at my teammates. But the tracks indicated the VC moved slowly away then hesitated several times to look back in my direction before moving silently on.

This cat and mouse game continued until I had driven the three men out of the bamboo thicket onto a rudimentary dirt road that bordered a small thatch hut village. The three men managed to reach the protection of the village where they melted in with the local inhabitants. I knew it would be foolish to pursue them into the village and I felt guilty for leaving my teammates with even less protection than we started with.

I turned back to the imposing bamboo thicket knowing I had to once more wind my way through this dense concealing maze. Once again I had to look high and low for any booby traps as well as any hidden VC It may sound crazy but this type of large bamboo was so dense that a person could easily walk within a couple of feet of another stationary human and never know they were there.

Charlie had become quite adept at hiding

in such places but with some luck I managed to find the opposite side of the thicket, coming out in full view of my teammates who were just completing their work.

The burlap package was heavy as it contained packed dirt and blocks of TNT and as we discovered later upon opening the package, some form of white powder. Was this a dress rehearsal for a chemical attack? We never knew and the threat of chemical attacks lessened until nearly forgotten.

Before departing we showed the security team our findings and explained the explosive catapults operation. But they were more interested in trying to persuade us to accompany them to a large clearing where a valuable battalion sized VC flag was staked out for anyone brave enough to take. The idea was foolish, if not suicidal to begin with and it was made even worse by the fact they wanted us to disarm any booby traps, then seize the flag so they could make it their war trophy. Our answer was a flat "no" especially in light of the fact that this team had refused to provide security in their own back yard. A man would have to be crazy to trust such a group of men and that thought remained in our minds in all future dealings with this security team.

GARBAGE CANS

The Viet Cong were an ingenious adversary. They made do with what was at hand, often making weapons of wood or bamboo or even using our discarded soda cans for grenade bodies. The improvised products were necessary because their supplies came through North Viet Nam by way of the Ho Chi Mien trail. Tenacity must have been their by-word because the Ho Chi Mien trail stretch roughly 300 miles from North Viet Nam through Laos and Cambodia to the Mekong River Delta. This trail covered some very rough inhospitable country made up of jungles and plains where muddy was the normal road condition.

The mode of transportation could be by truck but often times it was caravans of bicycles or much of the time movement was on foot. All the material required to make war in South Viet Nam was pushed or pulled or drug by human muscle through the mud down this remote trail.

If all these impediments were not enough to stop the movement of goods on the trail you must add in the attacks by our bombers, helicopters, and ground forces. Now if you think I am pleading a case for sympathy for the VC you couldn't be more incorrect. When you make war on a group of people it is beneficial to know as much as you can about them. Underestimating an adversary is asking to lose in any field of competition but underestimating an enemy can prove to be deadly.

A case in point was the two rockets we faced in South Viet Nam. The larger rocket was the Communist 122 mm rocket, which weighed 101 pounds, was 75 inches long and 4.8 inches in diameter. The 122 mm rocket was a fin and spin stabilized weapon with a range of 11,000 meters, plus it incorporated a two position nose fuse, one was instantaneous detonation on impact while the other allowed for some penetration before detonation.

The other and more common rocket was the 107 mm which weighed 41 pounds; it was 33 inches long and 4.22 in diameter. It was spin stabilized with a range of 8,300 meters and normally functioned with an instantaneous nose fuse. The VC considered both of these weapons as their heavy artillery, especially in III and IV Corps areas. Both weapons had a long successful record when used properly, especially if fired from their launching devices. The problem being the farther south that material had to be transported, the fewer launchers became available. So Charlie once again became inventive by forming a launcher out of two boards nailed together in the shape of a V. This limited accuracy, as well as range which was programmed in before launch by Kentucky windage or rule of thumb but mostly by a "that looks good" attitude as Charlie adjusted his make-shift launchers. Many, many of these rockets missed their intended targets, often by a great distance.

Also most of these rockets were fired remotely by use of a cheap wrist watch or a can filled with water that dripped out water until the contacts were closed and the rocket was fired. This means of firing was employed because our artillery became very proficient at rapid return fire either day or night and it was usually at night that these attacks were launched.

I was fortunate enough to visit some of these launch sites and even collected some of the cheap watches and batteries used in these attacks. They were crude set-ups at best but they managed to function most of the time. Occasionally the EOD teams were called to render safe rockets or booby traps left behind by the VC gunners.

The smaller of the two rockets, the 107 had a warhead shaped like a bullet but the opposite end contained venturies that were canted to impart spin similar to a bullet or a football. This spin helps stabilize the rocket body and increases accuracy. Some part-time rocket scientist in the VC camp decided a rocket could do more damage if it carried a larger explosive charge. So this genius unscrewed the warhead, then sawed off the fuse and began welding together steel plates to triple the payload area. He then reattached the fuse well and the threaded mounting band that holds the warhead to the rocket body. He also attached a circular metal tail at the rockets base hoping to counter the angled venturis spinning effect.

Now I'm sure that this budding engineer was very proud of himself while any junior high science student could point out all the mistakes made in this design.

We began to nickname these misbegotten weapons as "trash cans or garbage cans" because they were so ill conceived. Some warheads were so bulbous that it was almost impossible to bring the nose fuse in contact with the ground, others had large bulges on one side that threw the weight off center, while other warheads were so long and heavy they threw the rocket out of balance and were nose heavy. The end result of firing these cobbled together projectiles is that they delivered very erratic flight paths.

The sound of rockets passing over was a fairly common and recognizable thing but the reinvented trash cans gave off a howl like nothing else in the ordnance field. The VC normally fired these creations at night so it was difficult to see how they flew. But if you were ever caught outside at night when a trash can passed over and we often times were outside, it's eerie sound was unforgettable.

I often times wondered if those poor VC who carried the 107 mm rockets on their backs down the Ho Chi Mein trail ever knew how their efforts were wasted by some moron who thought they had a better idea than the Russian engineers who originally designed and tested this fine piece of ordnance.

GARY JAY POOL

SELF PROPELLED 155

There has and always will be a rivalry in the military over who were the foremost artillery men, the Army or the Navy. I have lived with both and heard their point-counter-point arguments. I also had the privilege of witnessing both branches in action. I would declare the contest even except that the various military branches love to harass one another over most any given subject. This usually good-natured bickering is part of the esprit de corps that becomes part of every loyal military man's heart and soul. In a difficult situation I would put my trust in either group.

With that said, I must give a nod to the Army artillery if for no other reason than they possessed such a wide array of weapons and ordnance, far too many to list here. I enjoyed watching all of these guns as they completed their firing missions. But the 155mm self-propelled gun was one of my favorites. It was big, powerful and mobile, who could ask for more. When they fired the 155's the ground shook, dust flew and that was just from the propellant charge pushing the large projectile out of the barrel.

The self-propelled 155's were pretty sneaky and would move around at night to take up firing positions waiting for a live fire mission. One of the places these huge weapons like to reside but unknown to us, was a clearing very near to our building. Then some time later they would receive a fire mission and those big propellant charges would fire, resulting in a huge ka-boom, a sound that would wake the dead.

The new men in-country would yell "in-coming" just before they rolled out of their bunks to land with a loud thud on the hooches plywood floor. The more seasoned men would remain quietly in their beds having long ago learned the difference in the sound of in-coming and out-going artillery. The in-coming rounds produced a sharp crack from the high explosive detonation which was a signal to all to hit the deck.

The new men usually took some ribbing from the old-timers for their error but they soon became seasoned vets who would calmly remain in bed while the self-propelled crew went about their business.

A WILD GOOSE CHASE

People often ask what a typical bomb call consisted of in South Viet Nam. My answer has always been, "there were no typical calls and very few similar ones." A team might respond to two or three leaking white phosphorus rounds in one day and then not see one again for two weeks. Some calls were reported by soldiers who had no idea of the potential hazard of say, small arms ammo as compared to an actual booby-trapped hand grenade.

One non-typical call came in early one morning from an infantry unit down in the Delta who reported a booby trap in their compound. My teammate and I were given the assignment which we eagerly accepted even though we had no idea of where this unit was located. Our clerk was usually very knowledgeable as to unit locations and which roads to take, what routes were the safest and where to go for help if things got out of hand. But even he didn't know exactly where to find this call and as it turned out no one else in our unit had any real information.

Time was slipping away so my teammate and I loaded up a jeep and headed out in search of a booby trap. We followed what few directions we had been given, along with some wild guesstimations while racing down a well-traveled main black top road into the Delta. We located several dirt roads that led to who knows where and finally settled on the one that was the more well-traveled thinking heavy traffic would lead to an Army unit.

This single track road was narrow and rough with a lot of foliage growing up nearly blocking out our view. Where I come from this road would be called a cow path, although other than water buffalos I never saw any bovine in South Viet Nam so we decided some other critter had made this trail. Such roads were a poor place for two men in a jeep to be traveling unescorted but this was common practice in most Army EOD units.

We encountered a small convoy of duce-and-a-half trucks moving slowly in the opposite direction and what with the road being so narrow we gave them the right-of-way. A jeep running rear escort paused long enough to report they had no idea of our missing unit. They also suggested that we turn around and follow them out of the area. But our typical hard-headedness prevailed so we proceeded onward.

We spent a great deal of time roaming up

and down roads that we couldn't find on our maps. We couldn't pick up our unit or any other units on our radio so we stopped what few people we encountered along the road hoping for some easy direction to our destination.

We finally rolled into a very lush valley where the hillside was covered with banana trees and, this being midafternoon and we hadn't eaten all day, it was decided to pick some of the small low hanging fruit. Of course, this was in direct disobedience to the Army warning to avoid all food and drink other than what the military provided. But the area had not been defoliated so we had little fear of ingesting Agent Orange, however these short ripe native bananas didn't taste like those purchased in the grocery store back home. We agreed it had been such a long time since either one of us had tasted a real banana, or strawberries or nearly any other fruit for that matter, that our taste buds were playing tricks on us.

After our impromptu lunch we ran across some soldiers standing in a group some distance from the dirt track road. The whole thing looked peculiar but we finally managed to get one man's attention and he slowly approached our jeep. We told him of our situation and after some thought he declared a new unit had moved in up the road a couple of klicks (Army slang for kilometers).

We thanked the man for his information

and were careful not to ask what his buddies were doing standing around in a circle. There are times when it's best not to ask too many questions of grunts out in the field. Ground ponders and the like lived in a different world with their own little pass times, games and entertainment. I had ventured out into this jungle to dispose of a hazardous booby trap not to play the role of an MP.

We followed the soldier's directions and drove on for a couple of miles only to come to the end of the road. There wasn't a soul in sight, no noise, and no smells (and there were a lot of unusual smells in Viet Nam) so we turned around and drove back to the cluster of GI's.

We hoped to make one last attempt at locating our mysterious unit and its booby trap so we parked the jeep and walked the short distance to where the GI's were still standing around in a small circle.

One of the soldiers called and waved to us to hurry up or we would miss all the excitement. As we drew nearer it was clear these troopers were gathered around a large homemade cage. This in itself was not unusual for in our travels we had seen caged monkeys of many different varieties, large lizards, little honey bears, and any other critter that these lonely GI's thought strange and entertaining.

This cage contained a very large python

snake and again that in itself was not unusual but the ten or twelve excited men told us of our good fortune to be passing at this very moment. It seems the snake's owner had the reptile on a very restrictive diet of one feeding every two to three weeks and today was the day.

It's funny how these strangers were so excited about sharing this moment with us, they openly invited us to stay and even included us in their humor about the upcoming event. Most of the jokes center around one young black soldier that the large snake kept his eyes on. If the soldier moved around the cage the python's big head followed like a magnet and a piece of steel. The group of soldiers told the black man that they thought the snake was partial to dark meat, something that couldn't be said today. The young man took all of his buddies jesting good naturedly and was quick witted enough to point out the snakes response to some of the other men.

Shortly one of the men approached carrying a young pullet that was quite upset at being handled. The man opened a door on the top of the screened-in cage and dropped the squawking nearly grown bird inside. We all expected a lightning attack but the python never moved a muscle, instead he remained frozen in place until the pea brained fowl calmed down.

In just moments the bird climbed up on

the reptiles back and proceeded to walk around, pecking at the enemy's slick skin. This waiting game continued on for a few minutes until the chicken walked in front of the snake's head and then like an explosion, the attack commenced. The large snake opened his mouth as wide as possible while grasping the bird on its right side, the pullet made one small squawk as the reptile wrapped it's massive body around it's own head and it's victims body. The whole attack took only seconds as we all stood thunder-struck by the snake's lightning speed and strength, while we were all astonished at the birds in ability to recognize a deadly enemy under its own feet.

Nothing happened for several long quiet minutes as the snake lay coiled around it's supper like a large green spring. Then ever so slowly the muscled body began to relax, until the ball of white feathers came into view. Once uncoiled and with the chicken's dead body still locked in the powerful jaws, the snake lay very still obviously recuperating from it exhaustive capture and kill.

Getting back to business we asked once more for the location of our reported booby trap with one soldier offering up a possibility just up the road. We took our leave from the friendly troopers who continued to ask us to stay and be witness to the pythons devouring of his prize but duty called and we moved on.

Once again the trip and the road turned into a patch of overgrown jungle so we returned to the sight of the chicken's demise for a quick chat with the group of soldiers. They welcomed us warmly and insisted we watch the now rested snake as it slowly engulfed its meal. It took some time for the reptile to completely devour the feathery body, head, feet, wings and all. By the time we said our good bye, the pullet was nothing but a large lump part way down the reptile's body and it was clearly still moving.

The daylight was fading as we pulled out with no idea of how to get back to our base. Traveling the trails and back roads in this area at night was never a good idea, but we had been out of contact with our base for most of the day. We were offered and could have spent the night with the soldiers at the gathering but again no one knew of our whereabouts. Many of the roads and highways had a curfew at night as well as did the gates into many of our bases. It was decided to just blunder along and with some dumb luck we would manage to get home without being shot.

It was well after dark when we talked our way through the back gate at Long Binh post, it took several explanations as to why we two were off post after dark but we finally arrived at the 3rd Herd. Now, one would expect a warm welcome for two men missing all day long but to the contrary and as usual we were interrogated by every member of the unit, their thinking was that we had snuck off to party somewhere. I asked if the unit had been shorthanded in our absence but they replied that it had been a quiet day. I then asked if anyone had tried to find us or radio us but they admitted only a couple of attempts had been made with no results so they gave up the effort.

I was tired and hadn't eaten except for a few bananas all day so after I gave them a sound cussing, I went to bed knowing I could not prove where I had been and they could not prove anything we had done wrong. But during the night I got to thinking this whole affair, bomb call, road trip and all might just have been another of the First Sergeant's attempts to keep me away from the building or to lose me altogether. The next morning I thought that was crazy until I learned that no one had written down the information or name of the unit we were to visit plus we never heard from some disgruntled Sergeant demanding to know why we had not responded to his call.

Now I'm not pointing fingers at anyone, in the first place I had five or six First Sergeant's and four or five Commanding Officers, not to mention other Sergeant's above me who might have planned this little excursion into the boonies as a practical joke which was quite common in EOD units. The call might have been the dream of some of the local druggies, of which there were many. It is quite possible the whole affair was the product of my over active imagination.

I will be the first to admit that I am an out-spoken individual, with opinions that are not always looked upon with favor, my mouth has always been my worst enemy when dealing with people. However, after this incident I watched what was happening in our unit and it was decided by mutual agreement that it was better for all concerned if I was out of the building. So I volunteered for any and all calls that came in regardless of what or where they were reported. This meant that some team members were reluctant to be teamed with me while others were of the same mind and were glad to be out in the field.

Me with a 107 mm rocket

DEADLY PILE

On this particular call my teammate and I were not out on the loose for a change, our destination being Bear Cat Base only a few miles down the road from Long Binh. We received many calls from this small but active base. This call differed from the others in that it was not an emergency but rather we were told it was to inspect and destroy any dangerous items in a VC arms cache that had been very conveniently moved from the jungle to the fire base. This sounded like an easy day, no slogging around in the mud or fighting through heavy jungle foliage.

Upon arriving at Bear Cat Base we were directed to an open area near the perimeter wire. We had expected a small cache of ordnance, instead we found piles of explosives. It was clear from our first glance that the men who delivered this cache had absolutely no idea of safe explosive handling, or the proper segregation of such material. There were piles of loose granulated TNT, five gallon open topped cans filled to the brim with hard recast explosives that had obviously been melted out and recovered from our bombs. That was all right in itself but in the same proximity were piles of fuses and initiating devices that contain very sensitive explosives.

The cache looked like someone had backed up a truck and thrown everything off as if they were delivering a load of firewood or empty sand bags, there was no rhyme or reason to the placement of these hazardous materials. My partner and I visually inspected the cache trying to make a plan for the safest way to remove and destroy this disarrayed pile of ordnance. A plan was quickly agreed on, it being to first remove the most sensitive items from the conglomeration hoping to prevent our tripping on or dropping anything on these touchy items.

Just days before this call we had been warned by headquarters of an incident where a live fuse from a PG2 or B-40 rocket propelled grenade had accidently been knocked off a desk top at a height of approximately 30 inches, this fuse was normally seated in the base of the Communist manufactured rocket propelled grenade's war head. The fuse was what is known as GI proof in that the soldier firing this weapon did not have to pull out safing pins, or make any settings or adjustments to the fuse. The individual simply fired the weapon from his shoulder launcher, then ducked. The fuse had a firing pin that was restrained from striking the very sensitive primer by the use of a coiled spring. The truth is this weapon and fuse combination were very effective being engineered in such a way that if the grenade impacted nose first or on its side, the fuse would initiate the explosives. Add to that the explosives in the fuse was very potent if detonated alone and if you listened closely the spring retained firing pin could be heard sliding back and forth inside the fuse body, that is if a person were foolish enough to mishandle this fuse. Don't ask me how I know this.

We got right to work, each man picking up and removing the more hazardous items that were closest to the entryway. There just happened to be a pewter plate containing a pile of the in-question fuses, some twelve in all, of B-40 fuses that were not restrained in any way. The plate although sitting on open grass was surrounded by piles of flaked TNT as well as loose black powder so I called dibbs on handling this item, which my partner was more than happy to allow.

I squatted down in front of the plate full of fuses and carefully grasp the edges of the battered metal plate before attempting to rise. As I stood up I could feel the presence of something soft, wet and clammy on the bottom of the plate.

Snakes! Poisonous and nonpoisonous were everywhere in South Viet Nam, that was the first thing that flashed through my mind. My second thought was a scorpion, a brother to the one that stung my left hand a couple of weeks before and left my whole arm numb for hours, plus the memory of the intense pain of that now dead arachnid was still fresh in my mind. So I instinctively reacted by raising the pewter plate to eye level in order to view whatever critter was wrapping its body around my fingers.

With the plate now above eye level all I could see was the fingers of both of my hands being engulfed by some brown creature. But true to our bomb disposal training, I remained calm making every effort to discern what type of critter was pinned between my hands and the plate of explosives. It was then that I heard one of the cylindered metal fuses from the top of the pile begin to roll, it struck several other fuses before landing with a clank on the lip of the plate. I knew there wasn't anything I could do to stop the fuses travel because if I released my hold on either side of the plate to catch the moving fuse, others would be thrown off of the edge. The metal to metal sound of the fuse striking the plate was like that of someone bouncing on a diving board in preparation to make a dive. I just knew with my luck the explosive fuse would never land on the edge of the plate and stay there, no it had to roll off the edge in the direction of my face. I watched as if in slow motion as the fuse dropped by my eyes then my nose, followed by my chin before disappearing past my chest. Still I knew I couldn't risk moving the plate full of fuses or trying to move away, I would just have to stand there and hope the odds were in my favor and that the fuse would land on its base, the only place that it was not very likely to detonate.

I'm not a gambler so I don't know how to figure the odds of that fuse landing on the one out of three possible sides where it wouldn't detonate. Still holding the plate high and steady, I looked down though my out-stretched arms in time to see the fuse land between my feet and I swear I could hear that striker compress its retainer spring then slam back against its case.

"Watch what you're doing," my teammate stated in a calm unflustered voice before turning back to the task at hand. That fuse had dropped a good five feet before striking solid ground between my feet without detonating, which would have set off a chain reaction of the high explosives scattered all around us.

Realizing that nothing had detonated and that neither one of my hands had been attacked, I sheepishly picked up the wayward fuse and placed it once again on the plate before exiting the pile of explosives. Once outside, I carefully placed the sensitive plate in a safe place then reluctantly began to examine my hands. Suddenly a powerful stench filled the air and I knew immediately it was coming from my hands.

Of course, a person's natural instinct is to place your nose close to the suspected odor and inhale deeply just to be sure your senses are still working correctly, mine were.

I wiped the foreign substance off of my hands before returning to the cache pile and there on the ground was every evidence that some practical joker had relieved his bowels, then placed the plate and fuses on top of it knowing that some dumb GI would place his hands under the plate and into his excrement.

It was a hard lesson for an arrogant EOD man and one that could have proved fatal to my partner and myself. But we looked under and around every item in the deadly pile of explosives before picking up or moving anything else for the remainder of that day.

MALARIA PILL

I was sitting around with several vets the other day, shooting the breeze about our time in service when I mentioned the mandatory malaria pills we were forced to take. A couple of the guys said they never took any malaria pills in or out of country and didn't remember ever hearing about such pills. I got the same response from a couple of the other guys except they did recall people complaining about the pills. It's truly amazing what fifty years can do to a person's memory.

I began to wonder what war these guys were in because the subject of the malaria pills came up once every week when we were forced to take them. Nearly every mess hall in-country had some Sergeant standing at the exit making sure that every GI ingested his two pills no matter how hard they complained or what excuse they gave. Our unit was a little different because our work schedule prevented us from eating in our battalion mess hall (thank God) on Mondays.

We were to take our pills on the honor system but one of my First Sgts. never took them because they made him sick. Other members of our unit took the medicine occasionally, others just lied and said they took the pills. For those who don't recall this practice, try to recall that you were issued enough pills to take them religiously for the next six weeks after returning to the world.

Why all the fuss over taking this medicine you might ask? Well, often times after taking the pill you had the same symptoms as having malaria, sometimes even worse. Nearly everyone got diarrhea at least for the first day of taking this pill, some heard the call for two or more days, while rare cases had nausea or other side effects. If allowed to, some men cut the pills in half stretching them out through the day, while others went with fourths but some places would not trust the GI's to take the issued pill so they were forced to get sick.

Some poor fellas were just beginning to recover from the bouts of diarrhea when Monday rolled around again. That meant a whole year spent in an outhouse in a tropical paradise.

The antidote for this malaria pill was good old pink Pepto Bismol which came only in a liquid form from glass bottles, not the handiest thing to tote around in a combat situation. It was not unusual to see a vehicle slide to a stop even on main roads and a GI would hop out, roll of toilet paper in hand, and head for any type of cover. In some cases they didn't even try to make it to cover. Often times the poor suffering GI didn't have a roll of toilet paper, he just carried the few tiny little sheets of toilet paper supplied in the famous C-ration pack. Then of course some GIs weren't even lucky enough to have even that brown paper wrapped gift from Uncle Sam.

There was a fairly large outhouse located near our building that we have many times watched some unknown plagued soul come out of nowhere, pants half down racing for all he was worth to reach the sanctity of that grey poorly vented six-holer in time. To some of these men that run-down, foul smelling place was a blessing straight from heaven. Every GI's golden rule entailed never to deny another GI the use of their units outhouse.

Still the whole matter was one of pride to the individual soldier because the citizens of Viet Nam had no qualms about needing privacy, they stopped wherever they were to answer nature's call and they thought nothing of interrupting you inside or out when your turn came.

I guess those awful pills may not have prevented malaria but they did bring together two different cultures on at least one common ground.

FIELD EXPEDIENCE

Maybe I should have titled this book Two Men Lost in a Jeep or My Vacation in a Foreign Country, where you can't speak the language and half of the population wants to kill you. Some of my closest friends think our EOD teams were escorted to and from incident calls and that a guide would greet us with a cold drink and a fan to cool our sweaty brow. But nothing could be further from the truth, maybe some of the other branches operated that way but not the U.S. Army.

A team would be handed an assignment with its general location and possibly some directions and if the Sergeant in charge smiled, you'd best write a short letter home telling your family how much you loved them. On the way to your jeep someone would invariably call out asking if they could have your new Seiko watch if you failed to return. Of course, that started everyone else present to calling dibbs on your bunk, your new camera, or stereo.

All of this jesting was considered good natured fun but thinking back to some of the calls we responded to, this chatter might have been in earnest. Still frivolity and humor is the crutch a lot of men lean on while at war. It's better to have a sense of humor than no sense at all.

In this case the Sergeant who gave us the call nearly broke out in fits of laughter while the other team members called out dibbs on everything we owned including our underwear which no one wore to begin with. My partner and I waved at our teammates as we drove away from our building but without saying a word we exchanged knowing glances.

It took some doing to locate what we thought was the correct booby trap but in Viet Nam a person didn't have to look far to find a suspect piece of ordnance. Finding and working on the wrong booby trap was a common occurrence but we decided if it was not the correct one, it looked like one we would like to try.

This booby trap was located far out in the bushes on what was the remains of an old plantation. Heavy metal fencing and masonry foundations were still visible in what appeared to be a work area. The IED was a 155mm high explosive artillery projectile that had been placed on its side in a hole in the ground with its base

192

plate against a brick and concrete foundation. Only the fuse well protruded out of the ground and the fuse had been removed with a large wooden hand carved plug in its place. Two holes had been drilled in the wooden plug, a 6 inch long piece of blue wire had been inserted into each hole. The wires were not connected to anything but merely stuck out in the air. My partner and I went through the usual precautions checking for any type of anti-lift or anti-disturbance device, but nothing was found. Still we were reluctant to brazenly pick up the projectile fearing the possibility of a secondary explosive device had been placed under or behind the base plate.

It was decided that we would move the projectile remotely and in those days that meant a long piece of rope was used. However this jeep only had a short piece of rope about twenty feet long and twenty feet is far too close when a 155mm projectile detonates. We began to scrounge around the plantation but only came up with a few feet of old rusty wire which we looped around the wooden plug sticking out of the projectile's fuse well.

Our accumulated rope and wire gave us about 50 yards of clearance which was not nearly out of blast range if the projectile should detonate. Then with what seemed a stroke of genius we tied our belts, web gear and rifle slings together but we still lacked a sufficient standoff distance from our booby trap.

We had early on eliminated the idea of placing C-4 on the projectile and do what was known as blowing it in place. We had rejected this idea because the explosive would have to be fired non-electrically which means several minutes of delay between the time we lit the time fuse and the detonation. This was often a tricky business in that anyone or thing could walk into the shot after we called fire in the hole, especially knowing that with just the two of us on site we couldn't control the area. The only option that seemed feasible required our moving the projectile remotely to see if it would explode when moved. Of course, looking back nearly fifty years, I realize our best choice would have been to leave the job and never look back. But that old bull headiness and the thought of some poor innocent person finding the projectile and accidently killing themselves on it overrode our own fears.

So now we had a plan, maybe not a good plan but having even a bad plan was better than not having any plan at all. We tied every piece of rope, cord, or line together that we could find but we were still inside of the blast radius of a 90 plus pounds 155mm projectile.

We had discussed hiding behind the remains of a building's footing which stuck up about two feet above ground level and was close enough that our Rube Goldberg rope would reach that far. However we were still inside of the blast radius, something neither of us cared to witness up close and personnel. We knew if we used the concrete and brick foundation for cover the blast wave from a detonation that size could prove very painful if not lethal. I tried to persuade my partner to find a safe place to hide but he refused as always saying he was as much to blame as I was if anything should go wrong.

So we hesitated and talked everything over once more as all good EOD teams were taught to do. As Art Macksey, an old partner and very experienced EOD man used to say, "there is always time to die, don't get in a hurry."

Suddenly the quiet of this beautiful jungle scene was shattered by a couple of rifle shots just to our right. Those shots had come from what we guessed were about two hundred yards to our east so we were well within rifle range but we were certain the bullets were not meant for us. The first reports were easily identifiable as 7.62 Chi Com rifles, very likely AK 47 rifles although the shots were not full automatic so the weapon might have been a Chinese SKS rifle.

We made our weapons ready as we waited intently for any further sights or sounds but we knew this was a game changer for us. A few seconds that seemed liked minutes passed before more 7.62 bullets were fired and this time we could tell the weapons in use were full automatic AK 47s which usually meant VC Those rounds were followed by full automatic fire from 5.56mm M-16 rifles which probably meant some of our people.

Now if you are sitting there thinking that I'm crazy saying we could identify the difference in the report from these two weapons, let me assure you the difference is like the song of a canary in a cage or a Bald Eagle screaming as it circles over your head. Both sounds are derived from birds but they are entirely different and immediately recognizable. Men in the field in Viet Nam quickly learned to identify these two weapons reports and those of many others because it could mean the difference between life and death.

It was now clear that a good sized firefight had developed out of nowhere just a few yards away and from the sounds the game was moving our way. We had no idea of who we were dealing with, what their allegiance was or if they even knew of our presence. There wasn't time for a long discussion so without saying a word we both dropped down behind the concrete foundation and gave our make-shift rope a yank. But nothing happened, no detonation or other sound and we quickly discovered the home-made rope had stretched under the weight of the strain. I wrapped a couple of feet of the line around my hand then pulled again fully anticipating a detonation but again nothing happened. Cautiously peering over the foundation, we could see the projectiles steel body standing on its base plate.

Without a word we jumped up and raced to where the 90 pound 155mm projectile stood like a guard protecting his assigned post. We gathered up our rope and as the firefight grew more intense and closer we grabbed the explosive round without checking any closer for booby traps and ran to where our jeep was parked. Once the projectile was loaded and secured in place, we raced down the back road wondering if those involved in the firefight had any inclination that the two of us were within a hundred miles.

All the way back to the base we laughed at Navy instructors at the Navy's EOD school who were so strict about calling different size ropes by their proper terminology, like a string, a rope, a line, or a halyard, wondering just what they would think of our rope made of rifle slings, and rusted wire and canvas belts. We finally decided those instructors would pronounce the whole mess as a field expedient, something they all took great pride in assembling.

GARY JAY POOL

ASSASSINATION TEAM

The idea of being lost may sound nonmilitary or nonprofessional but as I have often stated the combination of strange names, both Vietnamese and military produced a lot of confusion especially for those of us who were less than world travelers.

A call came in reporting an unexploded 750 bomb that was located in the Delta. The U.S. Air Force jets were the origin of such large bombs, some were duds while others were dropped unarmed from planes that declared an in air emergency, this allowed for a safer landing. This was often termed pickling the bomb load, which meant the device was dropped by the aircraft but were not armed. The VC loved to locate such weapons, armed or not, because these bombs provided a large amount of reusable explosives.

If Charley could locate these bombs first one of their members would volunteer to hack saw through the steel outer shell of the ordnance. On occasion the VC would set up a movie camera to document the man's bravery, several people would shake hands with the volunteer then quickly depart as he went to work. If the volunteer should succeed without a detonation all the well-wishers would rush back into the camera frame and congratulate the man for his great deed. The volunteer's only payment or reward was the large red silk rose that was pinned on his chest. That's not much of a reward for the amount of risk that he had taken.

Once the bomb was sawed in half Charley would turn the ends of the bomb case forming a large V at the center. A pit was then dug at the apex of the V and a fire would be built against the bomb case. The fire melted out the hard cast explosives and they slowly drained into the pit where they cooled and solidified, being recast in whatever shape the hole had been dug in.

At other times the melted explosives were drained into open topped five gallon cans for easy transportation. In either case we liked to detonate these bombs to prevent the VC from harvesting the explosives which were used to make IED's and large claymore mines.

Three of the members of the 3rd Herd EOD were given the assignment to travel into the Delta, locate the bomb and destroy it. The exact location was unknown and no guides or security would be provided. We quickly loaded up our fastest M1-51 jeep Number 44, it would run over sixty miles an hour plus it had a pedestal mount in the back where you could mount an M-60 machine gun.

One man drove, one rode in the front passenger seat armed with an M-16 while I manned the M-60 from the back seat. Not following proper procedure, I was also armed with what was known as a CAR 15 which was actually a short barreled M-16 with a collapsible shoulder stock. The weapon proved to be much handier when deployed from a vehicle or when disarming mines or booby traps, because an EOD man carrying a M-16 would often times have to place the weapon out of reach while disarming a mine, which is not a good alterative. The CAR 15 was short enough it could be kept on the EOD man's body where it would be ready for use in an emergency. This shortened version of the M-16 has now became a standard issue weapon for many combat troops and although they were scarce in Viet Nam, once I acquired a CAR 15 it went everywhere I went.

Our driver that day was a good wheel man, always alert and looking for action. The passenger was also a good calm dependable man so I felt relaxed and ready for a restful scenic Sunday drive.

Old Number 44, called our "gun jeep" was the fastest of the unit's three vehicle fleet. Old Number 44 would peg out the speedometer's needle and on a good day it would pass that magical point sometimes running 65 mph. This excess of speed came in handy when the speed limit on most of the modern highways in South Viet Nam was posted at 35 mph, occasionally 45 was permitted. We being special with our vehicles decked out in red lights and sirens felt free to drive at full throttle, that is if you could keep those jeeps upright.

The M1-51 jeep had the ability to spin out of control or even roll over on even the slightest corner or road top irregularity. This vehicle had such a poor record that the Army required drivers to attend a special school before they were issued a separate license above that of a normally issued military license.

One of the property disposal lots or junk yards was located very near our building and it was always full of wrecked M1-51 jeeps with odometer readings from 6 miles on up. Of course, being within walking distance made it the prime place for midnight requisition for parts to keep our jeeps running.

With our competent driver at the wheel old Number 44 made good time as we three raced along highway QL 4 headed south. We sailed through large rubber tree plantations before breaking into wide open rice paddies. I leaned back while taking in the sights and thinking this is the way wars should be fought.

We had traveled several miles into the flat Delta rice paddy area when I looked down the road far enough to see a small motorcycle approaching. Being an old motorcycle fanatic, I looked at and envied every Vietnamese who rode these Honda 50cc step-thru motorcycles right up to those mounted on the really powerful 90cc models and there were literally tens of thousands of these little two wheeled banshees on the roads.

My interest in motorcycles caused me to sit up from my restful reclining position in order to get a good look at this quickly approaching motorcyclist. The road was a smooth straight black top and the rider was approaching at a moderate speed and seemed in complete control of his motorcycle.

We had closed to less than one hundred yards when the man and motorcycle crumpled up and fell to the black top. Our driver slammed on the brakes and I jumped behind the pedestal mounted M-60 machine gun without knowing what had taken place other than it was an usual accident.

Our heads were on swivels as we scanned the vast open rice paddies for any sign of danger when two Vietnamese men began to rise up out of the green knee-high rice plants approximately fifty yards to our right. They held up their weapons and cried out chu-hoi which indicated they were surrendering or were friendly, it was a universal term that even the least experience GI should have known. But I wasn't sure because they had just gunned down a person right in front of us.

The two muddy men clad in black pajamas waded across the rice paddy to the road while calling out phrases I didn't recognize. The men appeared friendly and relaxed as they stepped up onto the road then waved to us before approaching the dead man long enough to give him a couple of traditional swift kicks.

They approached our jeep while trying to explain they were an assassination team that had been ordered to kill the high ranking VC, it was obvious the two men were quite pleased with their efforts for the day.

I, being a suspicious type, never took the barrel of the M-60 off of these men for we had no way of knowing if they told the truth or if we were to be the next target on the hit list. And at the sake of sounding cowardly or a nervous nelly, I came very close to cutting them in half as they rose up out of the mud. But as I have said, when the band strikes up a tune and the lead starts flying everyone present begins to dance.

This was a country where the good guys and the bad guys looked and dressed alike, sounded alike, and might even change sides depending on what time of the day it was. It was considered bad form to initiate a gun fight especially if you didn't know how many players the opposing team had hidden on the bench.

I'm not sure even some 50 years later if we did the right thing but a few polite smiles and congratulations and we were on our way South once again. My eyes remained on the two men behind us as we sped down the road. Of course, it should go without saying but I will say it, everyone, especially the man on the M-60 stayed awake the rest of the drive. We stopped sightseeing and put our cameras away and no matter how hard we tried we never did locate the 750 pound bomb we had been assigned to destroy.

GARY JAY POOL

MEETING THE AUSSIE'S

Travel in Viet Nam could prove exciting and sometimes deadly for the inexperienced traveler. My partner and I were told to respond to an incident far down in the Mekong River Delta but again little information or direction had been provided. So we began to load a jeep, and as usual one man grabbed the C-4 while the other gathered up canteens of water, cameras and film along with our tool belts and placed them in the jeep just before we jumped in the front seat. Our First Sgt. was nearby casually leaning on a post that supported the building's little porch roof.

"Forget anything?" he asked in a nonchalant voice.

"No," we replied looking around the jeep and the equipment that might be needed.

"You two going on an off-post call?" he

inquired matter of factly.

"Yeah," I answered pleasantly.

"Then where are your weapons?" he demanded with a growl as we turned off the jeeps ignition and slinked back into our sleeping area to retrieve our weapons. It was a good start to a long drive through the hot tropical Asian countryside.

We laughed at the First Sergeant's way of seldom giving orders, he'd rather try to make you think of your error. His system usually worked and he was usually right but we would sometimes commit such common errors on purpose just to make him think he was needed in the unit. It was all a game, some Sergeants didn't understand our humor as well as this First Sgt.

Once loaded and armed we hurried down highway QL 1, talking about how to find the location of this incident. But try as we may by driving down one lonely back road after another we failed to locate our incident site.

After a brief discussion we continued south along Highway 1 hoping to stop a convoy or a MP patrol to ask directions. As the jeep topped a small hill we could see several men in the distance moving along the shoulder of the highway. The men were unrecognizable from our point of view and as we seldom encountered large numbers of VC on the main roads in broad day light, still stranger things have happened. We slowed down while silently rolling closer to these mysterious individuals and I was thankful the First Sgt. had shamed us into bringing our weapons along. Moving closer, weapons at the ready, we realized whoever these men were, they were not Vietnamese. Their walk was different as they moved along casually. Suddenly my partner recognized the four armed men as Australian soldiers.

There were two men walking single file on each side of the highway so we drove up between their rows and began asking questions. While friendly, they kept moving forward. They explained the four were the rear guard for a company that had just walked eleven kilometers through open rice paddies to find this road. The American forces would have been moved by some type of vehicle, most likely helicopter. We quickly explained our dilemma and they admitted to having no idea where they were, but their officers were about a half mile ahead and they had maps of the area. We thanked the men and offered them a ride to where the rest of the company could now be seen taking a break. They refused saying the other men had walked it and so would they. I urged the four men to ride along but they continued to refuse until I explained I wanted them to introduce me to the CO so we could see his maps. It didn't take long for the rear guard to crowd into our little jeep once they were given a reason to ride along.

We caught up with the Australian company, about one hundred men strong, who after that long hot, muddy and exhausting overland march were wrestling with each other. Some were chasing a couple of dogs, others were playing catch while a few of the soldiers were sitting in the grass and resting. True to the rear guard's word they introduced us to the CO who showed us maps of the area and yet we still could not locate our site.

I noticed as we walked back to our jeep that several of the young Aussies were watching us very intently but seemed reluctant to approach us. Just as we started to get into the jeep one of the four men from the rear guard stepped forward and asked if he could see my rifle. It was a CAR 15 which is a shortened version of the M-16. My partner and I were always reluctant to allow anyone, friend or foe to handle our weapons but I reasoned they had us out numbered 50 to one so I removed the CAR's magazine, racked the bolt back to eject the round from the chamber, then handed it to the man. He looked the weapon all over as a small crowd began to form, each man wanting to handle the short stubby rifle. They began to twirl the rifle by its trigger guard like a handgun saying something about Josh Randall, the lead character from the TV series Wanted Dead or

Alive. It was quickly explained that Wanted Dead or Alive was a popular TV series in Australia at that time, 1969 which was about ten years behind its air dates in America. Most of the Aussie men were armed and carried the FAL, a large long heavy weapon that weighed around nine pounds, that plus all of their gear made for some difficult hiking.

This seemed like a fine time to give up our wild goose chase and head back to the unit. Once again we failed to find our objective but we saw a lot of different roads and met some nice people so the whole trip seemed well worth the effort. But I often wondered if no one knew where any other unit was located how did they avoid stumbling into friendly ambushes, or calling in air strikes on each other. But then that wasn't my job, I was in-country to defuse bombs and booby traps not to plan troop movements.

I want to add that I or we made friends with the Australian EOD team that was in and out of Long Binh. I became good friends with an Aussie named Sgt. Smith who dropped by often to drink (drink is not the proper word for these men, our 3.2 beer was like baby formula to them.) and exchange views. Several members of our unit wanted to do some trading with these men from down under so I mention this interest to Stg. Smith and he arranged with one of their members who was known for his bargaining skills to set up shop in our office. The man arrived the next evening with his goods. He had Kangaroo leather boots, military coats, and of course their famous hats with one side folded up. It seems the Australian military would not allow their soldiers to take home any items issued by their government but they were free to ship home anything issued to the American soldiers, such as jungle boots, ponchos, poncho liners, jungle hats, and jungle shirts.

Sgt. Smith and I sat in our bar and talked as the dealings began but in a short while one of the younger men came in and sat down. I could tell by his long face that something was wrong and when asked he was reluctant to say, until another soldier came in complaining about the Aussie trader's unreasonable rates. In a heartbeat Sgt. Smith and I were on our feet headed for the office to confront the man about his high binding ways. The long standing rule of our building stated if you brought any outsider in and he caused a problem or started a fight you were considered directly responsible.

Sgt. Smith and I burst through the door together but he spoke first and in a loud clear voice he explained to everyone's satisfaction what the going rate of exchange would be in this shop. The trader began to disagree but Sgt. Smith took a couple of steps closer to his man and explained that we were American EOD personnel and that he was Australian EOD and that is not how EOD people treat one another. It was clear the trader would rather take a beating on his merchandise than a beating on his body. Now that the prices were set and locked in Sgt. Smith and I returned to our bar where he apologized repeatedly for his man actions.

The Australian troops were as well known for their fighting ability as they were for their drinking prowess. I soon learned this Aussie had a reputation among his own troops as a fighter and that few chose to offend his independent way of thinking. But he was always polite and jovial around us and I never saw him threaten anyone. He did divulge to me his real name and several questionable facts from his past. I guess he trusted me with this information, why I don't know, but I never told a living soul, as he said that is not how EOD people treat one another. I had vowed not to make public his secret and that's how it has remained.

GARY JAY POOL

WHITE MICE

All right now tell me if you have heard this one before. I and a Staff Sergeant were told to go to a place named Dong Tam; it's best described as a mud hole on the Mekong River. The Navy had a base there on the river's edge, the Ninth Infantry (Army) had occupied part of the area until they were transferred bag and baggage to the north. Our unit was assigned to pick up some of the slack from the EOD unit that was also being moved. Dong Tam was located so far from Long Binh that we had to set up a temporary duty (TDY) station at the old unit's building.

The Sergeant and I hooked a trailer to our jeep and started loading it with everything we thought would be needed for a two week stay in the Delta. This was mid-morning and the Sergeant had already been drinking and was becoming very belligerent and demanding.

The intoxicated Sergeant demanded that he drive and after a heated argument that I lost, we headed off post. His driving was bad and his attitude was even worse, he displayed a lot of what is now known as road rage.

As we reached the outskirts of Saigon he announced we had to visit the EOD unit stationed there and again we argued but he refused to listen to common sense. We were already running late and some stretches of the road were dangerous for two men to drive alone in the day time not to mention what they were like at night. No matter how much I protested we ended up in front of a French Villa that housed the EOD unit.

We nearly exchanged blows after leaving the jeep and trailer filled with both our personal and military possessions unguarded along the well-traveled street. But he demanded I accompany him into the house to their private bar so that he could buy me a drink. He and the unit members knew I didn't drink but he did and continued to do so as fast as the bartender could punch two new drinking holes in the top of the beer cans. At that point of his inebriation the First Sgt. at the bar nodded his head towards the door and whispered, "get out to your jeep first and whatever you do, don't let him drive."

I hurried out to the jeep and sat down behind the steering wheel to wait for the Staff Sergeant's return. I have no idea how much more the man drank during the next half hour but he was roaring drunk and mad as hell when he finally returned to the vehicle. He gave me a direct order to let him drive or else I would face a court martial. The threats and yelling continued for several minutes until I told him to either get in the passenger's seat or be left behind. The unrelenting verbal abuse could be heard by the other motorist as I weaved my way through the heavy traffic.

As we approached a heavy traffic corner there was a policeman directing traffic with hand signals from a podium in the middle of the intersection. It was at this point the Sergeant decided to get out and walk back to the unit we had just left. It was quite a wrestling match trying to keep him from jumping out in the middle of a busy four lane street.

The South Vietnamese police were called White Mice because they were attired in a white shirt and hat as well as white gloves. Most of these White Mice had a superiority complex and they meant business. My drunken Sergeant and I were still wrestling in our moving jeep as we approached the White Mice traffic cop who had signaled for all vehicles going in our direction to stop. I complied with his orders, still trying to hold the Sergeant in his seat until the traffic cop waved his pretty white gloved hand for everyone to proceed through the intersection. This street was a wide four lane and I was driving on the inside lane next to the White Mice's podium as we moved through the intersection and down the street in heavy traffic when all of a sudden a gun fired. I turned in time to see this protector of the people crank off another round in our direction.

I tried to push the overweight Sergeant down towards the floor of the jeep but there wasn't much room and he was still resisting my efforts to keep him safe. When another bullet from the White Mice revolver came our way I accelerated hard while trying to slide down under the jeeps steering wheel but the effort was in vain. It was only then that I realized our little jeep and trailer were being outrun by tiny Vietnamese women on Honda step-thru motorcycles, their hats and split tail pajama shirts blowing in the wind as they zoomed by us.

I never knew why that White Mice shot in our direction or if he did in fact hit anyone but it was not uncommon to witness such acts of lynch-law on the streets of Saigon. The Sergeant and I ran flat out until we rounded a corner and were out of sight of the lawman. I turned to the Sergeant to see if he had been hit but he had passed out and thankfully remained so for the remainder of our drive.

SAFING A GRENADE

We rolled into Dong Tam Base in midafternoon to find the streets lined with empty jeeps and three quarter ton weapons carriers. I couldn't for the life of me figure out why all of these vehicles were parked on this empty street and where all of the troops had gone.

I found the EOD building which was reportedly empty but three men and two dogs were still hanging on. I stowed our gear before asking about the jeeps lined up on the black top road, I thought they were to be transported north to rejoin the Ninth Infantry. But that wasn't the case, the jeeps were what the Army called mavericks or stolen vehicles that had been remarked with unit designation and then put to use.

Shortly after that the Army published some figures showing how many thousand maverick vehicles were in-country and how many thousands of gallons of gas they burned every month. I immediately put through a call to the 3rd Ord explaining the situation and wanting to know if we could use another jeep but they declined so I was forced to drive around all of these abandoned jeeps for a full week.

The second night we were in the Dong Tam EOD building and the night before the two remaining Sergeants were to leave, they got drunk. I don't mean they just drank, no they got belly crawling drunk and began to demolish the building. It had a long covered veranda on one side that had good florescent lights, decent tables and chairs, something that our unit didn't have. When asked why they were demolishing all of this, they told me they had built it so they could rightfully tear it down.

I got a chair and without interrupting the fun, sat back to watch these men destroy every table, chair and light bulb. One large man began to carry a good sized dog around by his tail with no complaints from the beast so I assumed it was a common practice. The party continued until there was nothing left to destroy, although they were coming up with some pretty inventive ideas that included the use of explosives and some military property. I managed to deter these plans and kept the two men drinking until they became too intoxicated to pull off their grand plans and finally fell asleep.

The two rowdy men were soon gone but the third man remained behind, sort of in limbo. We were instructed to never take this young man on any type of bomb call, he wasn't to drive any vehicles nor handle firearms. Those who knew said the young man had suffered a breakdown of some type but the Army didn't want to send him home fearing it might make matters worse and cause embarrassment for all concerned.

This nice looking young soldier was very pleasant to be around, always willing to help with any tasks that came up. Still, he would get into good natured mischief like playing backwards the tape of a reel to reel recorder that belonged to a man who vowed death to anyone who would touch his new machine.

The brass warned that we would be held accountable if harm should come to the soldier, but he often disappeared during rocket attacks, no longer fearful of their destructive power. He had a reputation for pulling pranks on other GI's, again having no fear of the consequences. This concerned me as we were absent from the unit most all day and part of the night. It was like having a new puppy at home while you were at work, there was no way of knowing what he was up to in our absence.

One evening while TDY at Dong Tam a message came in requesting EOD help at the scene of an ambush on a truck convoy. My two man team was on a call but fortunately another team was in the area and responded in our place. However they hadn't been informed of the restrictions on our young soldier and with them not knowing the way to the ambush site, were not only willing to accept his offer to volunteer to come along but also to drive the other team to the site.

When we returned and got the messages about the ambush and that another team was already on site we stood by just in case they had any trouble. It was getting dark and was about the time that the VC liked to mortar our compound but we hadn't any idea where our young soldier had disappear to. As time went by and darkness and mortars began to fall, I became extremely concerned for this man's safety.

Worried, I looked everywhere within the small base confines thinking the young man would never leave the compound, but he was nowhere to be found.

Shortly, the other EOD team drove in and there in the driver's seat sat our wayward trooper. The three of them began to relate the happenings of the call. It seems an Army convoy was ambushed in the center of a small village, one truck was destroyed and a firefight developed, the EOD team arrived just as the fighting ended. They reported ordnance scattered about the area, some of which was very sensitive and were armed. When they finished telling of cleaning up the ambush site, I informed the other men about the restrictions on our private's duties and they were surprised saying, "we thought he had stayed in the jeep during the cleanup and didn't think he handled any of the explosive items." As things calmed down our young soldier called me aside saying he had a problem that only I could handle.

The young soldier and I were standing just outside our building when he began to tell his account of the evenings call. It seems he was staying with the jeep while the team was busy disarming the hazardous items scattered about the village buildings and street, when some of the local Vietnamese approached him explaining there was something laying on one of the flat topped roofs.

He tried to alert the other two men but they were busy and the civilians became insistent that he do something about the explosive device. The young soldier foolishly followed the civilians behind the buildings. I say foolishly because he was unarmed and there had been VC fighters in the area just moments before. Charlie loved to get an American alone, out of sight in the dark and capture or most of the time kill them. But our young soldier was lucky, the villagers were more concerned about the hazard on their roof.

The young soldier found enough junk behind the building to produce a make-shift mountain that he climbed high enough to see over the roof's edge. In the dark he could make out the shape of a hand grenade laying on the flat roof. It seems it took some mountain goat blood to climb to the rooftop but sheer hardheadedness won the day, once more allowing our young friend to reach his objective. It proved to be an M-26 American made hand grenade laying on its spoon with the safety pin missing.

For those who don't know American issued hand grenades, they come in several body shapes and sizes but the fuses look pretty much the same but there are many, many model numbers of fuses. The standard fuse screws in the end of the grenade body with a sheet metal lever or spoon that runs down the outside of the body.

When the device is thrown the lever is thrown off by spring pressure and at the same time the same spring drives a striker to hit a cap-like primer that lights the few seconds of delay before the grenade detonates. On the older fuses a distinct pop can be heard as the striker impinges the cap, the new fuses are nearly silent. If a person walks up on a grenade that doesn't have a safing pin but the lever is still in place you have no way of knowing if the striker has moved or is ready to move or function.

Our young soldier had no way of knowing

especially in the dark what condition the hand grenade was in other than the spoon was being held down by the weight of the grenade itself. EOD men learn to pick up suspect U.S. grenades by holding the spoon tight against the grenades body then carefully wrapping black tape around the spoon to prevent it from moving.

Our young man picked the grenade up in the proper fashion only he didn't know if the striker had moved or was moving which would give the soldier four to seven seconds to get rid of it before it detonated. Also our man didn't have any black tape or tool pouch and couldn't contact the other two men to come to his assistance. Realizing he couldn't climb down from the building's roof one handed he became very inventive. He was wearing an expansion watch band that he slid up and over his hand using it in place of tape to hold against the lever and spring.

Most EOD men carried flechette nails or even the hand grenade safing pins in their hat to be reinserted in an event like this. Our young friend failed to follow this standard procedure.

He then placed the jury-rigged grenade in the upper pocket of his jungle fatigue shirt allowing him the use of both hands to climb down safely. When the team was ready to leave our soldier forgot to tell anyone about the device in his pocket, in fact he drove several miles back to base with the grenade in this condition.

The reason he called me aside as he pulled the grenade from his pocket, watch band still in place, was to ask me what he should do with the explosive device. I had several thoughts as to what he could do with the grenade but I quietly took possession of the device while one of the other EOD helped me remove the metal expansion watch band before we could safely tape the spoon down.

The other two EOD men suddenly became aware of the fact they had just ridden several miles over rough bumpy roads with a hand grenade made safe only by an expansion watch band and the cloth of a jungle shirt.

DEEP SORROW

My partner and I had been assigned to catch a helicopter flight to a very remote fire base that was situated on a flat spot half way down the slope of a hill. This was not one of our regular stops but I remembered there wasn't much room at this base, just a small landing pad surrounded by guns and tents and wooden crates, the regular tools of war.

We were riding in our favorite air craft, a Huey helicopter. As we approached the landing pad another Huey became air borne to give us room to land. I noticed out the open side door of the Huey there was a lot of activity on the ground, people scurrying around just below us which made me think the base was under attack.

I was surprised as we continued to land because if the base was under rocket or mortar attack, I expected the pilot to pull up and get out of the bombardment. The pilot made a nice gentle landing and we stepped out of the side door to a cool reception, nothing too surprising there. We didn't hear any explosion or small arms fire so we moved away from the Huey's prop wash so that they could take off once more.

A young Sergeant came up to greet us and explained what our call was all about. I told him I thought the base was under attack by the amount of activity we saw from the air.

The Sergeant explained that one of the young Vietnamese boys who was like a mascot to the men had just accidently ran into a spinning tail rotor. The impact had split his head open and part way down his neck just like a meat saw.

It seems the GI's were running around trying to help the youth but he died immediately. We watched the stunned soldier's faces as they carried the boy away, a deep depression settled over the little camp and polite conversations were difficult to find. The stronger men went about cleaning up the mess from the accident while others attempted to return to their work. If you doubt the existence of PTSD, I'll bet the men who witnessed that death can give you a vivid detailed account of it to this very day some fifty years later.

We finished our call and were lucky to catch a ride on another Huey going our way. That base was not the place for outsiders to spend the night, the residents were in mourning for a lost friend.

BOMBLETS

I had the good fortune to visit Art Macksey, one of the EOD field's greatest men before his passing and we of course began to swap Viet Nam stories and I found his memory to be perfect except for one incident. He asked if I remembered the little village we visited way down deep in the Delta where we had the long conversation with the village chief. We had made several such trips together into the remote parts of the Delta. I usually did the talking while Macksey stood by listening to the conversation of the group of villagers who invariably congregated around these meetings.

This arrangement seemed backwards since Macksey outranked me and he knew the Vietnamese language far better than I did. But there was good reasoning behind our madness, in working this way Art could pick up what was being said about us, because we were not always welcomed in these backwoods hamlets. In fact, some of the villagers believed they were still fighting the French Army because they called us the people with big noses. I guess we all looked alike to these people, some of who had never heard of the French Army's withdrawal from South East Asia.

On one such trip the two of us were encircled by a large number of Vietnamese who murmured through my entire parlay with the village elder. After a few minutes Macksey nudged me from behind and whispered, "did you hear that guy? He is a North Vietnamese and he is a long way from home." I understood what Art was saying but I couldn't break off our negotiations so bluntly; it would look suspicious to the elder. After a little more talking, Art bumped me again saying, "there's another one." Still the elder and I continued discussing the problem at hand until I received another discreet nudge.

"God this places is crawling with North Vietnamese soldiers. Let's get the hell out of here," Art suggested in a calm easy voice. I nodded my head in agreement before giving the village elder a weak excuse why we were going out to the Jeep we had arrived in. We didn't hurry or show any fear but rather walked confidently to the jeep where we climbed in and waved a warm good-bye as we raced away.

Macksey explained that just like in America, the North Vietnamese have a different accent than that of their southern cousins. Besides he added, "they were making definite party plans for us once we left the village and wandered out into the jungle." I never knew Macksey to lie, or exaggerate for that matter, if HE believed there were NVA soldiers in that crowd, then I believed there were NVA soldiers in that crowd.

I had completely forgotten about the incident in the village full of NVA soldiers until Macksey began to recount it again. Several other stories were crystal clear in my mind but he recalled one that I just could not place until the end of his story.

It seems one day we flew deep into the Delta to a dirty run down little village where once again I began negotiations with the village chief who wanted his problem solved; a problem he reminded me was of our making. I listened to the village chief as he explained the Air Force had dropped some bombs that had become hung up in a tree near a trail his people used daily.

The chief was afraid to allow his villagers to walk on that trail for fear one of the bombs would shake loose and fall from the tree. He knew if the bomb landed as intended it would detonate, injuring or killing his people.

I admit I had a difficult time understanding the chief and could not picture in my mind a 750 pound bomb getting hung up in a tree without detonating first. When the old chief explained there were many bombs in the trees and used his hands to illustrate the size of these bombs, it became clear he was speaking of bomblets. I chuckled at the thought of 750 pound bombs hanging by their tail fins from a tree limb.

We soon discovered the chief's problem was some cluster bombs had managed to get tangled in a tree's limbs near the village without detonating. We had never heard of such a problem as these items had very touchy and dependable fusing systems. We had seen and heard of these items landing in an armed condition in certain muddy areas without detonating but never in a tree.

That is part of EOD work, any or every call can be that one in a million incident that no one has ever seen before but it's your job to figure out how to render it safe.

In order to aid the reader to understand this type of ordnance I will give a simple explanation of its operation. The US Air Force has a large inventory of what is known as cluster bombs, or CBU (cluster bomb units.) These weapons look like a normal 750# bomb covered in a thin tin skin with a seam running laterally around the device. When dropped from an aircraft they open up at this lateral seam, scattering hundreds of small explosive devices over a large area. As the bomblets fall through the air, the force of the wind moves or deploys fins or wings that arm the fuses so that when they contact a solid object it produces a detonation. There are many such devices yet they differ in operation, construction, and purpose. There are bomblets intended for anti-tank use, some are aimed at hard targets like bunkers but the anti-personnel bomblets have more and varied designs than any other category.

The bomblets we encountered on this call were ones known as BLU3B, or bomb live units or blue 3 b's for short or sometimes shortened even more to Bluies. They were shaped like a bell and were about two inches in diameter, they had a body made of pot metal like material that contained small steel balls to serve as shrapnel. The bottom of the bell had a round pressure plate that was held in place by several tin fins that were spring loaded. When the bomblets caught the air stream these fins folded up away from the pressure plate allowing it to drop down and arm the fuse. The fins also aided in stabilizing the device and bringing the pressure plate to land straight down on the target.

The offending tree in question did contain several bomblets that had become entangled in the tree limbs which posed quite a problem. If we tried to touch them the bomblets would fall and detonate probably causing others to fall and detonate. If we approached the tree any little breeze could dislodge a bomblet, or if some passing helicopter or other vehicle should pass near and cause a vibration we would have the same results, dead EOD men. Approaching the tree did not seem a good option but we could not come up with anything better.

Finally in desperation and being bullhead, I told Macksey that I could, from a distance, shoot the bomblets and knock them out of the tree. Of course, I meant from under cover but the shocked look on Macksey's face told me he intended to veto this plan from the start.

I must stop here to explain that as a youth I hunted squirrels every chance I got and I don't mean shooting those little tree rats when they were on the ground or when I was standing under their tree. I mean we shot them with 22 caliber rifles from a distance. Also I became quit good at shooting walnuts out of the tops of trees. In fact, I won several competitions with other marksmen in the area. But I could see from the look of terror on Macksey's face that this RSP (render safe procedure) would have to remain in the experimental stage as long as he was anywhere near.

Our answer to the chief's problem? Well, Sgt. Macksey explained in very fluent Vietnamese that the wind would eventually blow the bomblets from the tree and that we were leaving immediately. I never heard if the chief's problem ever got resolved but I knew full well that Art Macksey and I would not be present when it was.

GARY JAY POOL

SURGERY ON THE SIDEWALK

Late November 1969 Tex, Junior and I were called from our sick beds in the middle of the night to respond to an explosive incident. We three were members of the 3rd Ordnance Battalion ten-man EOD team stationed at Long Binh, South Viet Nam. Though normally only two men responded to such calls, we decided because of our illness all three should answer the call. The remainder of the team were either incapacitated or assigned to other calls.

Our only instructions were to report to a remote section of the perimeter bunker line where an explosion was reported to have taken place. Night bomb disposal calls, even if on base are much more difficult and dangerous to handle than those attempted in daylight. For security reasons many compound gates and interconnecting roads on Long Binh post were locked and guarded at night. Our compound for example, the 3rd Ordnance Battalion was one very small part of Long Binh post that had two gates that were closed at sunset. It was difficult even with emergency lights and sirens operating to make our way across the large base and through the massive ammunition depot to the incident sight.

On arrival at the incident site we were blocked access by the MP's depot security and the military investigators. When finally allowed near the sight, we found a dead American soldier who had been on bunker line duty that night. The large man's body lay face down in the dirt, his feet still inside the open doorway of an outhouse or latrine.

A large hole in the right side of his head just above the ear, combined with the M-79 40 mm grenade launcher laying inside the latrine told us what to expect. The military investigators allowed us to open the M-79 in order to ascertain by examining the empty 40 mm shell casing, which of the many projectiles this weapon could fire, was lodged in the deceased man's head.

Our findings were what we had feared, that the round was indeed a high explosive grenade type that Army regulations state **will never** be moved after firing. This regulation is due to the very sensitive fusing employed in the M-79 high explosive projectile. Standard render safe procedure calls for this item to be remotely detonated in place.

However, there is another military regulation that requires any explosive object that is embedded in the body of a U.S. personnel must be removed by a qualified U.S. medical doctor.

We then had no alternative but to transport this dead soldier with the high explosive projectile still buried in his head to the Medivac Hospital. This required loading the body into an ambulance then attempting to negotiate several miles of rough, rutted roads while driving with only black-out lights.

We loaded the body containing the explosive round into the ambulance and climbed inside the enclosed metal box that served as the rear body of the vehicle. We thought it best to support the body on top of our own hoping to cushion any shock caused by traversing the rough roads from detonating the M-79 explosive round. This trip from the bunker line to the Medivac Hospital locked inside the small confines of the bouncing hot, dark ambulance while holding a highly explosive dead body was a never ending experience from hell.

After a very trying ride from the bunker line we arrived at the hospital only to be greeted by what I would term as hostility. The facility CO, a Col. made it quite clear that he would not allow the dead soldiers body inside the building nor would he allow any of his personnel to touch the man.

We attempted to explain our position and the Army regulations that demanded a doctor had to perform the operation but he would not listen. We were finally allowed to carry the body inside for x-rays before being forced to return the deceased to the sidewalk outside the hospital's door.

Even though it was after midnight, a crowd of medical personnel began to gather around to listen to the on-going argument. However we remained in a stalemate for the Col. refused to perform the operation and we were prevented from completing our mission. We became inundated with questions and suggestions from those gathered around, none of which were productive.

This stand-off continued until a Lt. Col. wearing ordnance insignia materialized out of nowhere and began to ask questions. This officer seemed very knowledgeable about ordnance in general and the M-79 specifically and to our good fortune he backed up our statements concerning risks and regulations.

The hospital's Commanding Officer finally began to listen to reason and finally relented to the surgery, but refused to assign a doctor to perform the work. He insisted that whoever did the surgery would have to volunteer.

Fortunately for us, a doctor we knew was present in the crowd and he bravely came forward against the advice of his colleagues to volunteer for the surgery. He asked us to tell him the real risks involved and we admitted there was no way of knowing the condition of the projectiles fuse. It was made clear to the doctor that if there was a detonation during the procedure that we all ran the risk of losing hands, eyes or even our life.

To our surprise the doctor remained willing to perform the medical part of the procedure. The hospitals CO demanded the operation be performed outside of the building and that helmets and flack vests were to be worn. This started another argument because EOD teams at that time never wore protective gear. The Col. won out in the end when we allowed the doctor to wear a helmet and protective vest. Our team worked bare headed and in tee shirts.

We moved the body to a more remote section of sidewalk where we dismantled part of the hospitals sand bag wall to build a barrier around the deceased's head and shoulders.

We then pulled an ambulance nose-first up beside the body and directed its headlights onto a large mirror that we mounted on the hospitals exterior wall. We adjusted the mirror to reflect the light from the ambulance so that it would illuminate the dead man's upper torso.

When everything was ready, the doctor knelt down just outside the low wall of sandbags at what would be the top of the deceased man's head. Our team took up positions on top of the body in an effort to hold the head and upper body motionless and to provide instructions to the doctor as the surgery was being performed.

I had my right hand on the dead man's face when we realized his eyes were protruding grossly between my fingers. In a reflex reaction, I gently placed my left hand over my right in an attempt to force those huge haunting eyes back in their sockets. At that instant the doctor's helmet fell from his head and impacted directly on top of both of my hands and the dead man's head. The big steel pot impacted with a loud thud that made all four of us freeze in place and no one breathed for the next few seconds as we awaited the possible detonation.

Out of anger and frustration I stood up and with all my might, skipped the doctor's errant helmet across the black asphalt helicopter landing pad. My temper flared to the boiling point as I screamed profanities for all to hear that "just such accidents were exactly why we warned against wearing helmets."

The operation itself required splitting the scalp and holding it out of the way while we used a pair of pliers-like tool to break off pieces of the skull in order to enlarge the wound opening. We then took great care probing the inside of the skull in order to locate the exact position of the explosive projectile. This involved inserting our fingers inside the skull and feeling about the destroyed brain matter until we were certain of the position and condition of the projectile.

Once the item was located we quickly devised a plan for the projectiles safe removal.

We discussed the proper tool to be used in grasping the projectile's metal base and that it was imperative that once grasped, it not be dropped. The doctor pulled the projectile to the edge of the skull opening where our team took over. Once the explosive round was clear of the body, it was carried to the middle of the parking lot and placed in a pile of sand bags to await being transported to a safe area for detonation.

Just moments after the procedure was completed, medical personnel descended on the area and began taking photographs of the dead soldier's body still laying face up on the sidewalk. The military has strict rules against taking pictures of dead American service personnel with private cameras. We protested this activity to both the people involved and the hospital Commander, but he refused to take any preventative action. In the midst of this early morning excitement and reverie, one of our unit members arrived offering his assistance. This man was well known for his deep sympathy for our soldiers, especially the wounded or dead. His verbal protest of photographing a dead man soon escalated into a shoving match with several officers becoming involved. We were warned to intercede or charges would be filed against us. We managed to quiet the EOD man and to load the 40 mm projectile into the back of our jeep.

Our team returned to the building, wrote up the incident report and thought the matter closed. However a few days later, a number of officers arrived at the 3rd Ord demanding that our incident report be changed. It seems the investigators had ruled the young soldier's death a suicide while we had reported an accidental death.

Our decision came from examining the M-79 grenade launcher at the bunker line latrine the night of the death. We found the spring loaded swing-away trigger guard flopped from side to side exposing the trigger and that the manual safety was of questionable operation.

The young deceased soldier came from a poor black family who would be denied his life insurance if the suicide ruling stood. Not only that, but the deceased memory would carry a questionable stain forever. We had witnessed other cases where soldiers had been seriously injured or killed themselves because of horse play or senseless acts and they were given a medal and an honorable discharge.

In any case these officers gave us direct orders to rewrite our incident report, which we refused. They then ordered our CO to change the report but he could not because he was not present at the time. When all else failed, the orders became threats and bullying but we stood our ground and our original incident report remained as written. "Accidental Death."

OUT OF SHAPE

In the years since writing Xuc May, a number of things have come to my attention about the Viet Nam War. Many of those problems involve the poor or improper training provided to the soldiers heading into harm's way. I personally witnessed and have written about this subject repeatedly, some of these stories were humorous, others were deadly serious which makes me ask how many men perished because they lacked the proper skills to make a sound decision?

People have argued that the mistakes were not due to improper or lack of training but rather because the GI's didn't pay attention to those instructing the class or because they were unable to learn and process the information presented to them.

I admit those points are plausible but many of the errors I witnessed were committed by officers, young and old alike. The very people who were said to be the more intelligent of the military personnel, the men who were designated leaders, the ones you were supposed to trust for advice often times presented the most problems. I know anyone can make a mistake but many of these tragedies or near tragedies were the results of pride and arrogance not to mention sheer laziness on the part of those in charge. You can get mad if you want, but one of the stories I like to tell came about while I and a Sergeant were on TDY in the Delta.

We were called to helicopter into the Delta where we were ordered to jump out with all our gear from approximately 20 feet in the air. This doesn't sound bad unless you consider how much weight we had on and how deep the mud was in those rice paddies. I refused at first saying we were to be met by ground troops and there wasn't a soul in sight. Secondly the Sergeant with me was way overweight and out of shape, I doubted if he could even walk through the knee deep mud.

I was told to either jump or return to the base without completing the mission. So I jumped, finally coming to rest waist deep in muck and mire of what is considered some of the finest growing soil in the world. I was raised in Iowa so I would have to disagree with those experts who made that pronouncement.

I watched the Huey circling over my head as I tried to extract my body and gear from what seemed a cesspool of quick sand, knowing that my hard-headed, hot tempered Sergeant who was still in the helicopter was fighting tooth and toenail to prevent his being thrown out. He was demanding the pilot to land and the pilot was not about to set down in that quagmire. After some more circling, and I'm sure heated negotiations, the Huey descended down to where its skids were only two feet off the muddy waters. It was only then that my overweight partner crawled out of the helicopter and gently lowered himself into the mysterious liquid that the Mekong Delta was famous for.

The Huey disappeared in an instant, leaving the two of us waist deep in sludge with no soldiers in sight and we had no knowledge of where on earth we were. Our only option was to drag ourselves to the nearest rice paddy dike and wait for the infantry to arrive.

The time passed slowly as it always does when you realize you are a sitting duck for any VC who wanted to win a red silk rose or to collect the bounty money on our heads. My partner became more nervous by the minute, wondering where the infantry was at and questioning if the Huey had dropped us off in the right place. Being dropped in the wrong place had happened to me before and it's not too distressing as long as it's daylight but when the twilight descends across the rice paddies the shadows begin to take odd shapes and the call of the local wild life is reminiscence of the sound track from a Tarzan movie. It becomes clear you need to make a change. This situation was enhanced by the fact we didn't have radios or strobe lights with us. The strobe lights were employed in the dusk to signal helicopter or gunships that might come to your rescue.

We managed to hang on for a while then the sounds of vehicles could be heard, their tracks clanking their way through the gunk of miles of surrounding rice paddies. The A.P.C.'s (armored personnel carriers) soon surrounded us and began to unload troops and weapons. A few of these men were detailed to stay behind and protect the vehicles while we moved out.

The officer in charge who didn't wear any badge to expose his rank, (a common thing among officers and many NCO's in the field) fearing they would draw fire from VC snipers, was a long legged fellow who proceeded to set a fast pace down the top of a narrow rice paddy dike.

We went out a couple of klicks before the officer stopped to look at a map when his point man reported a booby trap ahead on the dike which I expected they would want cleared or blown up, but no, every one merely pointed it out to the man behind as we walked single file down the dike top. When it was reported we had gone eleven klicks from the APC's we made a ninety degree turn to our left then took up that line of march.

I knew my partner was overweight and out of shape and we were out in the open, exposed to the direct rays of the sun. I knew he was suffering the effects of this strenuous march so I asked if he wanted me to carry his forty pound demo bag and he willingly agreed.

Then suddenly we made another left hand turn and it was obvious we were headed back toward our APC's. This was like turning a tired horse toward his home barn, the men moved faster in anticipation of reaching comfort with less chance of being injured. In just a few minutes the young soldiers had left my partner and I and one other man who was the unit's rear guard in the dust, if there ever was such a condition in the Mekong Delta.

About this time I realized my partner was starting to have a heat stroke so we let him sit down, and gave him water and salt tablets while I moved his weapon and ammo to my load to carry. The young man on rear guard was armed with an M-60 belt fed machine gun with belts of ammo draped around his body just like you see in the action movies. This young soldier was understanding but obviously a bit nervous as we began to take up the trek back to the track vehicles. We hadn't gone far when my partner began to get wobbly and needed to stop once more and the young soldier could see in the distance his buddies had reached their objective, the parked APC's. I could sense his anguish as he tried to hurry my partner along but it was no use. We would wade through one paddy but as we reached the next dike my partner would have to sit down again.

The young soldier became very edgy and I knew he was going to abandon us out among the mosquitos and leeches and I also knew I could not carry my overweight partner and all of our gear without this young man's assistance. Finally in nervous desperation he blurted out that we had to hurry or they would leave us out here all alone. I reassured him they were not going to leave us and that we were perfectly safe as long as we had that M-60 machine gun along as company. It was at that moment that I heard the words I really didn't want to hear. "But you don't understand, I have never trained on an M-60, I don't even know how to load it," the young man exclaimed looking longingly at the dark forms of the distant APC's.

"That's all right," I said with a calm demeanor and an easy smile. "I can load one in the dark and I'm a fair shot with one, you just stick with me and I'll get you home all right."

That seemed to console the youth as he began to help me more as my partner became even more helpless. I asked how he happened to be assigned rear guard and didn't know how to fire his weapon. He explained that he had just transferred to this unit so no one knew what he could or couldn't do. I asked if his CO knew about this and if he didn't, would it be all right if I told him. The young man gave me permission to speak on his behalf and I did just that when we finally drug my partner up on one of the waiting APC's.

Officer or not, I gave him a piece of my mind for dragging us all over the Delta for a hazardous item that he couldn't find and to make matters even worse when my partner got over heated, he didn't send anyone back to help. Then I brought up the fact that his rear guard couldn't load or fire his assigned weapon, a common M-60, stating that matters should be looked into. I actually think this lowly E-5 had him worried because he became very polite and apologetic and I thought right there is the problem with this outfit, they had a weak Commanding Officer.

I had lost my temper and shouldn't have been so mouthy but the good officers I knew and respected would never have permitted such a lecture especially in front of his own men.

I was glad to take my leave of this unit just as soon as possible and I often wondered how they faired during the rest of their tour in-country.

GARY JAY POOL

MACV BUILDING

There were many things about that war that didn't make sense or at least prevented us from doing our work. Long Binh post was a large base, so big it was difficult to know every unit or where it was located. But while the rest of the post looked temporary, run down or military, there was one area where several large buildings of a more permanent style were located.

In this area was the Adjunct Generals office, or where the attorneys hung out. The interior of this building was as nice as any office building in any large city in the states. The Bank of America building next door was new and modern just like you'd find in downtown Kansas City.

Just down the street as I remember, was a tall brick building and again it was constructed of brick and very modern. This was the MACV building where all the brass spent their time. They had a general's flag hanging in front of the main door and we were supposed to salute it upon entering the building or so we were told. I was only in the building a few times but I always forgot to render a proper salute, if asked I would declare we were on a bomb call and didn't have time. This was normally true and to tell the truth I didn't care to be within a mile of the brass and I think the feeling was mutual.

I understand the building contained sensitive computers, which detonating our explosives even miles away caused the needle to skip on their phonograph. It was a problem for them but not for me, we were ordered to call in any planned detonation so the people in that building could prepare for the noise.

That rule had an exception, that being if the explosives were detonated in an emergency, and my shots were always an emergency. I can't say I was jealous of the people who occupied that clean modern dwelling and didn't have to eat hot dogs three time a day for six weeks, I just thought they should be outside helping the war effort. I'd hate to count the times I got reprimanded for setting off a shot without first notifying those people in their ivory tower.

One day we were tasked with destroying a variety of material, explosive and non-explosive, a job I dearly loved. As I have said before, we blew up a lot of knives and other items the Army deemed as contraband. But on that particular day we were told to meet some men in a truck at our demo range to demilitarize that load. It was a mixed bag of ordnance, weapons and junk that had been obtained locally although they never divulged the origin of this load.

My partner and I began to unloading the truck and with the help of the men we ended up with a nice tidy pile of material. One of the items to be destroyed was an old AK 47 that had seen its better day. It was covered with rust and mud and the wooden stock was full of shrapnel and had been on fire. The men with the truck began to ridicule the weary old weapon being certain that it would never fire. I challenged them to a bet, saying I was sure it would fire.

I checked the rifle over to make sure the barrel wasn't plugged and that the action was clear of large chunks of dirt and debris. I then recovered a really rusty and mud-cover full magazine from the pile we were to destroy and locked in the magazine well. I pulled back the bolt to put a round in the chamber then shouldered the weapon and fired four or five rounds on semi auto before I selected full automatic. I then fired the remaining rounds into a dirt pile. Once the weapon was empty I threw the old AK on the pile to be destroyed.

The men with the truck couldn't believe what had happened and I never managed to collect the bet but it felt good just knowing how dependable those old rifles were, it was a thrill to fire the old foe one more time.

Of course, I was once again reprimanded for firing a weapon in the demo area especially a communist weapon because it upset the depot security. But as I explained to the First Sgt. by the time security people arrived we could have been dead. It was a typical response, in fact we never counted on that group providing us protection, we always felt it would be us protecting the security people.

SMITTY TAKES A DIP

Late one night shortly after my arrival in-country, SFC Robert Smith woke me from a sound sleep to inquire if I would like to go on an interesting incident. Being new in-country I had been requesting to be taken on off-post calls. Actually I had been a nuisance trying to wrangle call assignments so I knew better than to refuse Sgt. Smith's offer even if it was late at night.

SFC Smith or Smitty as everyone called him had a very unique leadership trait that made it nearly impossible to refuse when he asked rather than ordered some task to be undertaken.

We quickly dressed, loaded in a jeep and headed off for parts unknown. The night being so dark and I being new in-country had very little knowledge of the area but I am certain we ended our drive at the Mekong River docks at Saigon. At the dock we grabbed our gear and stumbled through the dark to load on board a Navy Swift Boat. These brown water Navy crafts known as Swift Boats were fiberglass shallow-draft vessels that resemble the famed PT boat of

WWII fame.

The helmsman wasted no time in casting off before slowly motoring to the main channel of the Mekong River. Once the Swift Boat reached open water the helmsman pointed the bow downstream and threw the throttle wide open. The powerful motors roared to life and the large boat's bow reared out of the muddy Mekong water like a switch blade knife opening.

I will confess this ride was a bit unnerving yet somehow very exhilarating. The Asian night was very dark, as was the very wide Mekong River. The Swift Boat was also very dark and showed nary a running light as we raced over the turbid water. How that helmsman could see what lay in the waters ahead, I will never know but he never backed off the wide open throttle until we neared a very large boat anchored some distance from the river bank.

Smitty and I quickly transferred from the Swift Boat to the deck of the larger boat where we were led from the dark deck to the well-lighted bowels below deck. It was here that I learned the nature of our incident.

The all South Vietnamese boat crew explained in broken English that this craft was a river dredge. It's job was to keep river channels clear of mud and debris. This cleaning of the river bottom was accomplished by employing a large pump to suck the sediment off the bottom of the river. This MUCK was passed thru the pump then deposited onto the river bank.

Our problem centered on an artillery round that the huge pump had suctioned off the bottom only to become jammed in the large pump's impeller.

The South Vietnamese crew had opened up the pump far enough to determine the blockage was an artillery round but made no attempt at removing it. I questioned where the South Vietnamese EOD were but never received a straight answer. We got the usual double talk from the crew saying they could not understand us but at the same time insisting the round be removed immediately.

Smitty reluctantly agreed that we would remove the round since we were already on site. A brief discussion ensued as I quickly volunteered to go into the pump but Smitty insisted that it was his place. I stated that, being younger and single I should go but Smitty remained firm, not believing that married men should be exempt from dangerous calls. It was obvious I had lost the debate when Smitty began to strip down to his underwear.

I quickly reminded him that the pump was filled with river water that he would have to swim through in order to retrieve the artillery round. It went without saying that if the round should detonate while SFC Smith was inside the pump, he would have no chance of survival.

After stripping down to his Army issued OD colored boxer shorts, Smitty turned to me and whispered, "chamber a round in your rifle and if you see any of these crewmen make a move to start this pump, I want you to shoot them. I don't want to be chopped up and spit out in some mud pile," he said firmly looking me straight in the eye.

"I got you covered," I whispered back, hoping to relieve any anxiety he might have on that point.

He smiled and walked down to the opening on the pumps top. The muddy Mekong River's smell and appearance would have deterred many people from submerging their body into the pump, but Smitty settled in as if he were entering a hot soapy bathtub in some plush hotel. The Mekong River was a multi-use facility; the natives fished and bathed in its waters, but they also used it as a laundromat and a free flowing public toilet. I have witnessed South Vietnamese squatted at the water's edge brushing their teeth while just a few yards up stream another person was defecating in its contaminated waters.

Then without a word, Smitty took a deep breath and disappeared down through the blades of the pumps impeller. A few seconds later he re-emerged only to take another deep breath before sliding into the interior of the pump again. Suddenly Smitty hands, clutching the 105 mm projectile, broke the brackish water's surface. I gave a sigh of relief when Smitty's face, wearing a wide smile of pride also appeared into view.

I left my vantage point to hurry to the pump to take possession of the muddy 105 and to prevent any mishandling by the South Vietnamese crew members. I remember the crew did thank Smitty and praised his bravery for making their boat safe once more. I completely agreed with the Vietnamese crew but Smitty passed the whole affair off as a minor incident.

Now, if you share in Smitty's modesty then think about this; find an open septic tank and try diving 8 or 10 feet to its bottom and pull a 50# weight back to the surface. That is, without the chance of the pump starting up or encountering any one of a thousand other dangerous things that might have been concealed inside the pumps murky water. Now imagine the 50# weight you are recovering could possibly explode with any movement or the slightest impact.

We quickly secured the 105mm artillery round and made our way topside of the dredge where we found the Navy Swift Boat was returning out of the black to give us a ride home.

The ride back to the docks was a repeat of

the trip out except now I had more time to consider that this boat and crew were sitting ducks for ambush from the river bank or a floating mine in the water. I was glad to return to the 3rd Ord building and glad that SFC Smith pulled rank on me when he decided that he would be the one to dive to the bottom of that pump.

EQUIPMENT

I have recounted here and in other books and speeches about the difficulties we had in-country with procuring weapons. But I have said little about the Army side arms, especially the famed Colt 1911 45. Cal automatic pistol.

I was forced to qualify with the 1911 before leaving the states. The ten we had in our unit in the states were dreadful examples of the time honored old war horse. Their accuracy was non-existent, functioning was passable but they rattled like a baby's toy. The Air Force Sergeant where I qualified was not too excited about my shooting 45. Cal bullets at his targets that were designed for 38. Special.

When I arrived in-country we had a few 1911's on hand, they ranged in age from old to very old and from manufacturer to manufacturer, most appeared to be assembled from a rusty parts bucket. I tried firing them but they proved only accurate enough to hit the broad side of a barn if you happened to be standing inside that barn. Their sights were worthless as each projectile fired took a different course, some turned left out of the muzzle while others made an immediate right hand turn just past the front sight. We spent hours trying to reassemble these weapons in order to get one minute of barn door angle out of the selection on hand, remember the reworked pistols were considered the cream of the crop.

Many of us carried the famous 1911's in the field but they rattled so badly that you could not safely sneak up on a dead man. I always thought it good to carry these sloppy inaccurate beasts if only to make noise so the enemy would think you were returning their fire, might just as well been firing blanks, but the Colts were made of good steel providing a soldier with a handy sap or brass knuckle. But the best use I found for the 1911 45. was wearing them in areas where troops were not allowed to keep or carry firearms. A 45 on your hip or in a shoulder holster gave you a certain swagger status that these non-combatants could only envy but little did they know our 45's were merely window dressing to be used only at the last moment for intimidation purposes only because the target was normally safer than the shooter.

I was truly shocked upon returning to the world to find what a huge reputation these Colts had gained and continue to gain. In the last fifty years I have fought the urge to own a 1911A1 even with their new-found glories because I can still hear that metallic rattle they made as you walked stealthily through the silent jungle. The VC thought it was the good humor man coming to sell ice cream treats.

Another subject I have said little about were the knives that the GI's carried or for the most part didn't carry. The battalion area that our hooch was in prevented anyone from carrying a firearm or a sheath knife. Firearms were checked out from the unit armorer only when a person was going on guard duty, then it had to be checked in immediately after that duty ended.

Our EOD unit was exempt from these restrictive rules as we normally kept our rifles and hand guns near our bunks when not being worn. Most of us carried Marine style K-bar knives in a sheath on our web belts. These were often attached to the pouch that carried our crimping tool. This tool was similar to a pair of pliers except the jaws were made for cutting time fuse and crimping non-electric blasting caps onto the end of the time fuse. One handle of the pliers was flattened into a straight blade screw driver while the other handle was pointed and used to poke holes in explosives to insert blasting caps. When the handles were opened all the way we used the distance from tip to tip to measure time fuse.

Any knife found while passing through a

replacement company was confiscated and turned over to the EOD team to be destroyed. We often had foot lockers or trunks full of switch blades and sheath knives to blow up and sometimes it broke my heart to destroy these knives.

I was always a dutiful soldier trying to obey the rules but I felt that the long K-bar knives we carried and used mostly for digging around booby traps and mines left a good deal to be desired. I also acquired several knifes to be carried mostly out of sight, some small and sharp, others were big and heavy. The heavy knives only lasted a few trips into the field before I retired them for lighter thinner blades, it may sound crazy but it's all about ounces. I'd personally rather have more ammo, more water, or more food on me than a large steel bladed knife.

Our normal dress of the day was long sleeved jungle shirts with the sleeves rolled above the elbows during daylight hours as per military regulations. You were allowed to roll the sleeves down to the wrist after dark. There was never any sunscreen or suntan lotion available as we were promised and the Veterans Administration now blames the individual for having skin cancers. We wore jungle pants and jungle boots, the boots I liked and considered comfortable even if they did look like canvas covered clown shoes.

For headgear we wore either an OD baseball cap or more often than not, the wide brimmed jungle hat. A small wire was feed through the rim of the jungle hat to keep it from collapsing against your head but it could easily be folded up and crammed into your pocket in case of helicopter blades back wash. We wore a blackened EOD badge, known as the crab, on the front of our hats. Most men carried a few flechetts stuck in their hats to be used as emergency make-shift safing pins, also hand grenade pins were common, as well as that precious little roll of toilet paper saved from your last C-ration pack. The EOD badge was pinned to the hat and black rank insignia were worn on the shirt collars instead of cloth patches being sewn to the shirt which allowed the soldier to quickly discard such emblems in case of capture by the enemy. It seems they didn't honor our rank or status, it was better to be a common soldier if captured.

GARY JAY POOL

SHOTGUN SHELLS

One beautiful Asian evening my partner and I were left alone and in charge of the 3rd Herd, foolish people.

Suddenly two young soldiers in a jeep, pulling a quarter ton trailer, came flying up our driveway and slid to a stop, saying they needed an EOD man. So my partner and I looked at one another, then back into our building, as if we were trying to find an EOD man to assist these men.

The two inexperienced young soldiers were not sure what to make of us so we walked over to their jeep and asked what the problem was.

The two repeated that they needed an EOD man. It was at that point we realized the trailer was filled to the brim with shotgun shells.

"What's this all about?" I asked in a serious voice.

"Well," the young man who had been

269

driving the jeep began, "I work on the trap range and over the year I have policed up these once-fired Winchester AA trap load hulls."

"What trap range?" I asked, dumb struck to hear there was a trap range within a thousand miles of long Binh post.

The first young man started to give directions to the trap range, an area we had been to many times, so I shot my partner a questioning look. He replied with a shrug of his soldiers to say he didn't know anything about it.

"Who uses this mysterious trap range?" I asked.

"Oh, most of the officers shoot there nearly every week," the youth answered.

"What has this to do with us?" I asked, beginning to think someone was pulling a practical joke on us.

"My father owns a gun shop back in Ohio, so I collected up these once-fired AA hulls to ship back home as my hold baggage," he began to explain, a bit anxiously.

"I have four thousand empty 12 gauge shells in this trailer that I want to send home but I'm told I can't ship them without being inspected and certified by an EOD man," the young man paused then added, "worse yet I got my orders home and I'm nearly out of time."

The four of us stood around the trailer looking at the mound of bright red shotgun shell hulls, wondering just what to do with such an unusual treasure.

The young man was correct, any war trophy being shipped back to the states had to be certified safe by EOD. It was not unusual for some poor GI to show up at our building with a hand grenade or other explosive device to be certified by us.

There were times that the item did not meet the rules then in existence, other times the item was close to the guide-lines so we would offer to help. One of the standard requirements for inert ordnance to be labeled a war trophy called for at least a one quarter inch hole to be drilled at ninety degrees or on four sides of the body. This was to allow anyone handling the weapon to see the item was free of explosives.

"Four thousand shot gun shells," I stated in disbelief. "and you're telling me that every single one is empty and that the primers have all been popped?" I demanded, as I ran my hands down through the mass of plastic and brass searching for any contraband items.

"Yes Sergeant, I'm telling you the truth, they are all empty hulls with no live primers."

Both my partner and I were Spec 5, which is not really a Sergeant but we found that in many cases people would address us as Sergeant or Sarge to butter us up. They were trying to inflate our egos and it nearly always worked. In this case all we could do was take the young man's word that he had inspected each and every shell and that they were empty. My partner and I could sense the young soldiers desire to send the empty shells home. This was all he had to fill his hold baggage.

"All right," I consented. "I'll sign this form saying you have four thousand inert 12 gauge shotgun shells, but if someone is dumb enough to count these and they find 4001, we will both be in trouble or if one of them is loaded and goes off, knocking your plane into the Pacific Ocean, you'll have no one to blame but yourself," I teased the young man who seemed like a kid to us.

He and his partner thanked us several times before my partner explained how lucky they were because if some of the other EOD men had been present, the inspection certificate would never have been signed. We shook hands and they drove off into the magical Vietnamese night, never to be seen or heard from again.

I told my partner that I considered the kid as either the best liar or actor I've ever met but somehow I knew he was telling the truth.

My partner and I reported the whole story to our First Sgt. upon his return with nearly the same warning I gave the young soldier, except he said, "if it blows up your name is on the certificate."

But we never heard of any problems with unknown explosions or any air craft falling into the Pacific Ocean. It was just another day at the office.

GARY JAY POOL

BRIDGES

South Viet Nam was a land of rivers and canals. Many were, as I understand, dug by the French during their colonial days. All of these waterways were somehow connected with the mighty Mekong River which was a massive living creature that rose and fell with the ocean tide. Some hours the river was full to the bank edges while other times of the day wide black slick mud flats were exposed. Ocean-going ships sailed up the river during high tide to unload military cargo or to pick up raw rubber that was formed into big tan or dirt colored blocks for easier handling.

Being blessed with so many waterways, there were or at least had been numerous bridges. I say "were" because many of these fine structures had been destroyed by years of war. But some remained intact and were heavily guarded, often by South Vietnamese troops.

I always enjoyed taking new men across some of the old, very narrow bridges that were protected by South Vietnamese soldiers who walked back and forth across the bridge especially on the upstream side. It was their job to watch the water below for any sign of floating mines or sapper activity.

The Viet Cong would try to float mines disguised as trash downstream with the current hoping to detonate the explosives close enough to damage the bridge. Sappers were Viet Cong teams trained in the use of explosives. They were known for penetrating military perimeters and planting explosives where it would do the most good. The sappers had a reputation of infiltrating the impenetrable, they could crawl through rolled concertina wire with ease.

The soldiers that walked back and forth on these bridges would shoot at anything real or imagined in the water. I suppose the thought of someone blowing a bridge out from under your feet could make a person a little trigger-happy. Still it seemed they shot at things that were not there most of the time but in all likelihood these men knew far more about protecting a bridge than I did.

Why did I enjoy driving across these narrow one-way bridges with a new man, you may wonder? To tell the truth, it came from a dark sense of humor that many men acquire in a war zone. Often times the South Vietnamese soldier's guarding a bridge would fire their M-16 into the water below just as you drove by very slowly. The sudden report of a firearm right next to your ear got every passengers attention. I always thought the guards fired just as we passed to give us a thrill. In any case, nearly everyone would jump or call out with fright during these bridge crossings.

I also believe that part of this sudden reflex action was due to some of our troops being over trained in the states. They were told repeatedly not to trust anyone, civilian or military, old or young. This may have been a good piece of advice or a rule of thumb to go by, however it's difficult to distrust everyone you meet for an entire year. Many GI's took this warning to heart but unfortunately those people missed out on a lot of the sights and sounds of the country, not to mention the friendships we formed with the South Vietnamese citizens.

One way bridges where the Vietnamese guards fired into the water scaring individuals crossing.

DON'T GET OUT OF THE JEEP BOYS

I had the honor in my unit of being known as a person who took great enjoyment from the demolition or destroying of almost anything. This passion for destruction was greatly amplified if explosives could be employed in any part of the operation.

One beautiful day Junior, Big John, and I were told to go to our demo range and demilitarize a Deuce and a Half, a jeep and an Armored Personnel Carrier that had already been delivered to the site. It was just a coincidence that a large quantity of high explosives had been turned in to our unit also for disposal.

It seemed prudent to combine the operations and use the condemned explosives to demilitarize the three vehicles rather than draw new C-4 from stock in the depot.

We three hurried around loading wooden boxes of explosives into our jeep and trailer in anticipation of what should be an entertaining job. Blowing up something was always fun and getting away from the building just doubled our eagerness to get off base to the demo range.

Our jeep hadn't come to a complete stop at the demo range before Big John bailed out of the back calling dibs on the APC. That left the truck and jeep for Junior and me but we conceded the honor of demilitarizing the APC to Big John for he was as excited as a kid at Christmas when every package under the tree has his name on it. Big John in the mid-sixties was a strapping youth who lifted weights and never shied away from anything including work.

He fell immediately to the task at hand and began to carry box after box of explosives from our jeep to the APC. I paused in the midst of my own fun to ask, "just how much explosive do you think you need to destroy one big aluminum can?" for that's about all the American APCs were. He explained in mid-trip that we had to blow up all of these explosives so he would use enough to do the job right.

Big John, though younger than Junior and I was a proven EOD man with as much experience in demolition as either of us so we allowed him to continue setting his shot.

We figured the length of time fuse needed to evenly space the detonations, then capped up and primed our shots properly. With everything in readiness we scanned the area for any approaching personnel, called "fire in the hole" and ignited the time fuses before jumping into the jeep.

The demo area at Long Binh sat well away from the perimeter bunker line and although I never stepped off the distance it must have been better than a mile between the two. We drove at a moderate speed across the flat land that was entirely denuded of all plant growth while keeping an eye on our watches in anticipation of the detonations.

We had driven half the distance between the demo range and the bunker line when the first explosion came right on time; as did the second and everything appeared perfect until the third and last shot erupted with a huge roar. We all knew that this last detonation was Big John's shot that would send the honorable old track vehicle to where ever-faithful old war horses go.

The massive explosion was accompanied by the strangest whistling or howling sound that I had ever heard. Junior and I exchanged questioning glances then began to look in all directions for any sign that we were under attack. We had come under friendly artillery fire before but that had sounded entirely different. This new noise was not anything like the VC rockets that often roared overhead nor did it resemble any aircraft we had ever heard. I can only liken the sound to that of someone blowing into a huge pop bottle.

"Might have been an echo," Junior quipped hopefully, even though there was nothing for the sound to bounce off of for miles around. All three of us accepted in our own minds that the unusual noise was just one of those mysterious things that happen when one is in a war zone long enough.

Now I'm the first to admit that we should have returned to the demo range to evaluate our handy work but the three shots had gone off right on time and there was no question in our minds that the vehicles had been completely destroyed. So with a feeling of a job well done we hurried back to the building to brag about the enjoyable afternoon.

"Don't get out of the jeep, boys," SFC Smith called out with a devious smile, rising from his lawn chair that sat just outside the office door.

"Got another job for us?" we asked proud of the afternoon's work.

"A job yes; another call no," he began, still wearing that same smile that indicated something was wrong.

"You boys get those vehicles destroyed?" he asked candidly.

"Sure did Sergeant," we replied, beginning to wonder what he was leading up to.

"Good, now drive back down to the bunker line and police up your debris," his smile disappeared and his voice turned to a low snarl. "Seems you boys blew the side of that APC all the way from the demo range to the bunker line where it damn near hit someone!!"

A knowing look of shock passed between Junior and I as we suddenly came to the realization that the strange noise we heard driving back from the demo range had been the side of the APC passing over our heads. We naturally belittled Big John and hurriedly drove back to the bunker line. He, of course, insisted it couldn't have happened. But when we arrived at the bunker line we found the greater part of the side of an APC imbedded in the dirt near an occupied bunker.

The three of us quickly loaded up the large piece of metal, made a lot of sincere but hurried apologies then made a rapid retreat. The errant metal scrap was quickly returned to the demo range and it was agreed that the less said about the matter, the better. Still Junior and I often wondered why that piece of metal had separated from the rest of the vehicle and flown in the direction of the bunker line. We also wondered if Big John had planned this little joke; and if so, just how had he judged where and how to set the explosives to get the end results.

Now for those of you who are saying this scenario seems very unlikely; I recall an unsavory Sergeant who wanted a large teak tree blow down in such a manner as to make a foot bridge across a gully. The end results of that project found the tree blown down all right, but it landed in the opposite direction of the impassable gulley.

If one asks the right people you just might find out who placed the explosive on that wayward teak tree.

AMMUNITION DEPOT

I have said repeatedly that one of the most hazardous operations of any EOD unit was the cleanup after an ammunition depot detonates. The hazard is derived from the massive size of the depot and the huge variety of ordnance intermixed across the ground.

In an operating ammunition depot, explosives are separated by many different factors, the type of ordnance, its sensitivity, and compatibility with other explosives. Normally the segregated materials are, when necessary, stored in a pad contained within a U shaped berm or levy made of dirt about 10 feet high.

One end of the U is left open for easy access while loading and unloading trucks. However when ordnance begins to detonate it sets off a chain reaction that the dirt berms fail to contain. As a pad full of ordnance detonates, it spews its contents all over the area, some of which will land in another pad causing it to detonate and so on.

During the cleanup operations the EOD

men have to walk through piles of burned wood and charred, bent, melted or otherwise damaged ordnance that did not always resemble its original shape. Walking up on an issued piece of ordnance whether it ours or theirs is one thing but when you are standing in acres of blackened damaged trash you wonder where to begin. But someone always takes a deep breath then begins to carefully sort out either the most or the least hazardous item, then makes a decision on the best way to render it safe.

The common, but not always used, procedure calls for lining up several, usually ten or more EOD men nearly shoulder to shoulder and as they step slowly into the rubble all eyes are on the ground. They must look very closely at what is beneath their feet in hopes of identifying any explosive hazards. The line moves very slowly forward until an item is found. It must be quickly identified, then the finder must decide what dangers it might pose, not only to himself but the rest of the men in the line. If the item is safe, it is passed to the man beside you who then passes the item on until it reaches the exterior of the pad.

If the item is deemed extremely hazardous the man who found the device will call out a warning like grenade, leaking W.P. or whatever the danger might be. At that time the finder will pick up the item and step backwards out of line, never forward for in doing so he might set off another explosion. The line closes in and the man with the hazardous device moves to what is hoped to be a safe area to nullify the problem. Often times you are working with total strangers, so you must put your trust in their schooling, mental sharpness and nerve.

I was fortunate enough to spend two TDY's clearing the Marine ammo depot in Da Nang. It was a real mess that took weeks to clean up. I was also fortunate to work with some of America's finest EOD men on this job, many of the men were Marines who rotated in from outside of Viet Nam. They were not accustomed to the oppressive heat and humidity which made the hard strenuous work that much more difficult but they never wavered or asked to be relieved. Being overheated with nausea and dizziness doesn't contribute to fast, quick thinking while making life or death decisions, yet they pulled it off without complaint.

One hot morning we were in line moving in the direction of one of the remaining dirt berms when an explosion directly in front of us brought everyone to a stop, everyone's eyes on the berm ahead.

One of the men half way down the line yelled "grenade." He had picked up an M-26 hand grenade that appeared to be safe and intact but he heard the primer pop which meant he had four to seven seconds to find a safe place to deposit this hot potato. The man remained cool and without saying a word lobbed the live grenade over the berm where it safely detonated. We all got a good laugh at his belated call of "grenade."

We all knew if he had called out grenade someone would have bumped into him, preventing his throwing the explosive device or they might have ran in the direction he chose to make his throw. No matter how you figure it, that man saved possible death or certainly pain for himself and his teammates.

I often wondered if I had been in this man's place would I have responded as calmly and decisively. It's a question that fortunately never got asked, but I'm not sure after 50 years of thought what the answer might be.

Depot aftermath

This is what we had to search through looking for hazardous explosive items after the depot blew up.

ARMED AND READY

I was never one of the most loved members of the military. I often stated I would never win a popularity contest and never wanted that position, as I will illustrate here.

The 3rd Ord Battalion area was situated within an old rubber tree grove. These tall trees had long limbless trunks and were planted in a checker pattern, in other words no matter which direction you looked at them they were in a perfect row. Because of the even spacing of the trees this pattern made for easy maneuvering through the rows either on foot or in a vehicle.

When I first arrived, I was given a guided tour of our plush accommodations, the urinal - an old three foot long propellant charge can driven into the ground. The outhouse or privy was a six-holer, within easy running distance. I don't mean to be too critical of the Army's facilities so I will explain. The urinal did have a roof on it and side walls that extended about four feet down from the ceiling. This design allowed a person standing outside to determine if anyone was inside by looking under the sidewalls at the person's feet. This arrangement was not due to propriety but rather to prevent some hapless individual from walking in on a drug deal and getting waylaid.

The urinals and outhouses, even the bunkers were popular places for drug dealers to hang out or occupy. I was told during this informal tour that these facilities were to be avoided after dark and for good reason. More than one GI got into trouble for entering these illicit business places during their hours of operation. Many officers and top NCOs completely refrained from visiting these latrines either day or night by keeping some sort of slop jar in their rooms.

I or we never obeyed those rules because we usually carried a powerful flash light plus a side arm and called out a warning while approaching the building we intended to enter. This was not the militaries approved plan of action but I figured if the Army couldn't keep the lowly latrine safe for its members to use, we had little chance of winning a war.

I had just returned from a two week TDY to Da Nang when I made an armed visit to one of the facilities and as I rounded the darkened corner of our building, was accosted by three men who challenged my presence. They were carrying long clubs and became very verbal with their commands, mainly that I must go back inside our building immediately. I had no idea who they were or what they intended but I did know the Army regulations stated an EOD unit could establish a fifty foot perimeter around their building and that we were allowed to enforce this no-trespassing area if need be.

Their words became more heated as they insisted that I go inside and I told them in my most polite way that it wasn't going to happen and they couldn't make me. The men never identified themselves or their business or reason for being in our space. I also informed this trio that they were not allowed within 50 feet of our building without permission and I hadn't given them permission to enter. Well, push comes to shove and the standoff was about to end as they were armed with clubs and I was armed with a Colt 1911 45 cal. automatic pistol when Big John, one of our teammates came flying out the door and stepped in between the two sides of our little war.

It was then that I learned the battalion had passed, in my absence, an unarmed roving patrol of good guys to protect us from the drug dealers. Big John, who knew these three GI's explained that what I had told them was indeed correct, they were not allowed within fifty feet of our building, especially at night without permission. Then Big John explained that we all went armed and slept with weapons by permission of the Battalion Commander because we came and went at night in the manner of all emergency vehicles. He also explained that at times we were required to work outside in order to prepare for calls or to disarm an explosive device.

With that settled, I informed these men that I would not accept their presence within our boundaries at any time in the future. I told them every man in this unit would and could defend himself and their protection was not needed.

From that day on the unarmed roving patrols walked carefully around our building at night. The program seemed to fade away, as I was sure it would, because there were more bad guys in our area than good guys or at least good guys who were willing to patrol the area with the chance of being hurt.

I failed to make friends that night and many other times while in-country and yet some rules must be established and maintained if just for my own safety and satisfaction.

NCO CLUB

When I arrived at the 3rd Ord there was a nice wooden building with a pitched roof and screened-in porch located just behind and to the east of our building. I asked repeatedly its purpose but never got an answer. I thought it strange that every now and then some of the day workers would appear and begin working or cleaning this empty building but then the workers would vanish and no other activity could be seen for weeks until the day labors returned.

One day a couple of months after my arrival it was announced that the battalion NCOs were going to turn this building into their club. Although we had our own private bar known in EOD circles as the day-room attached to the back of our building, the drinking members of our unit whole-heartedly approved establishing a new NCO club. I being a non-drinker didn't have an opinion one way or the other. That is until it was decided that the access road to this new NCO club would be through our driveway.

I started out my disagreement by explaining that our little short driveway was for parking emergency vehicles and it was also used as a work area, as well as a mechanic shop for we did much of the work on our jeeps. I explained that at times a great deal of explosives were present in the driveway, not to mention some extremely hazardous items. I also argued there was a good road on the north side of the new NCO club that would provide them with unlimited access to a large part of the rubber tree grove that could be used for parking.

But no matter what my arguments they were bound and determined to use our driveway. I repeatedly stated I would not let that happen. But who am I, a low ranking peon to fight this cadre of powerful NCO's who did have permission to use the nice building for their club.

The argument raged on and on until one day several vehicles pulled through our driveway then across the open ground to the new NCO club. When a second wave of vehicles turned into our driveway I stepped out in front of them to stop their passage. Well you can imagine what happened.

This huge Staff Sergeant with biceps that looked like a weight lifter climbed out of the jeep and began to accept my challenge to put a stop to this once and for all. We yelled at each other long enough to draw a crowd and were just getting ready to start punching when one of my teammates thankfully grabbed me from behind and a couple of the Staff Sergeant's men grabbed him to end what surely would have been a bloodletting on my part.

I never knew what happened, it could have been a change of plans, or the Battalion Commander had a change of heart, or the NCO's thought better of the move, but when I left country several months later that nice pitched roof building with a screened-in porch still sat just as empty as the day I arrived.

Vietnamese working on NCO club

HARVESTING BOWLS

South Viet Nam had what was the remains of vast rubber plantations, many of these strange trees had been destroyed by the war or were neglected and abandoned to the Viet Cong. The South Vietnamese government tried to protect the rubber trees, calling them a natural resource.

I tried to teach a few of the members of the 3rd Herd to throw knives and axes and since our building was located in just such a grove, their long straight slender trunks made a passable target. However, the word got around and before long we or I was warned that damaging such a plant was considered counter to the war effort and the existing harmony that bound our two countries together, or something like that. The scolding was short and my memory was even shorter. I just made sure from then on that no one saw me impaling a rubber tree with a weapon.

Harvesting the milky white sap from the rubber trees is accomplished in much the same way that maple trees are tapped. A worker cuts a long narrow vertical groove in the bark to a point about two feet above the ground. The laborer then cuts chevron type slanting grooves in the trees bark which connect with the vertical groove.

A small white clay bowl is hung at the bottom of the vertical groove to catch the sap. These white bowls are glazed on the inside but not on the outside or the bottom. The bottom is round so it can be hung on the tree trunk by a wire loop.

The GI's liked these white bowls as souvenirs so I often stopped the jeep and wandered off into the rubber tree grooves to collect the bowls for those soldiers who did not have the opportunity to gather their own. However, it seems the U.S. Army, because of booby traps and snipers, took a dim view of this activity and the South Vietnamese government considered it plain old fashion stealing.

I couldn't understand their attitude because many of the bowls I harvested were old and hadn't held any sap for a long time. It was quite a thrill to wander alone through these deserted rubber tree groves where so many people had labored so hard to harvest rubber for our tires and door mats. It reminded me of my youth, sneaking through the hardwood timbers at home hunting squirrels with my .22 rifle, only now I was looking for white bowls and carrying a 5.56 mm rifle.

I must admit it was a bit eerie at times when looking down the checkered rows of trees and thinking you see someone moving from tree to tree and yet you knew it was only your imagination.

Being a good soldier, I curtailed this bowl chasing once it was made clear to me the error of my ways. That and the fact the old rubber in the bowls reeked to high heaven and was difficult to wash off your skin and clothing.

There are those who would disagree, but living as the enemy in that country could be a thrill a minute. A person only needed to find the right recreation and if Uncle Sam didn't supply the fun, a person only had to look about for entertainment.

GARY JAY POOL

MP'S

It's a fact that most GI's shy away from the military police or MP's, but just like our underappreciated police, they are here to help as much as harass. The 3rd Herd EOD had a good working relationship with most of the MP's we encountered, of course some were better than others. At times we had road races with the MP's, our fastest jeep against their armored cars. Both vehicles had red lights and sirens that we kept going as we chased each other down the nice blacktopped roads that wound through the picturesque but abandoned rubber tree groves.

This was considered great fun by both parties until Sgt. Smith got word of our impromptu road rallies. How he found out, I never knew and he wouldn't tell. He merely asked as we drove into our building parking area, "who won?" Of course, we played dumb but after the latest race, it was obvious that he knew the score which put an end to the races without another word or warning.

It was true the MP's had some hard cases

in their numbers who wanted to arrest you for doing your job. Others would let us slide by on a speeding wrap because we were friends. I have witnessed some of these MP's knowingly break rules and laws just like everyone else did.

L.B.J.

Long Binh Post was home to the famous Long Binh Jail or as it was better known L.B.J. the same initials as our famed president. This was a place to be avoided because they had some hard men in charge and their punishments could be very harsh.

I had the good fortune or misfortune to enter one small piece of this facility, the one where the prisoners filled sandbags and loaded them onto our truck.

There were guard posts on top of the wire perimeter where men with M-16s and pump shotguns watched every movement in this yard, often calling down to an individual prisoner to "move!" as they were required to run everywhere except when carrying full sandbags. This area was populated by what were called trustees, but I didn't see one single happy face among the prisoner faces. I don't think they found a great deal of joy in their work but I'm told it was better lugging sandbags than being in the hole.

I have often wondered why soldiers serving in-country would commit a serious crime. Think about it, to begin with, it's a very small country, one in which much of the population would be willing to take your life just because you are an American. Not only that, but there were four or five hundred thousand soldiers in-country that you would be forced to hide from. These same soldiers controlled all the transportation in and out of country except travel by foot or possibly waterways but even that was subject to search by armed vessel.

I knew a man who was obviously in distress, the typical symptoms, stomping, cussing, and throwing things. He was having domestic trouble at home in the states and he decided to go home. I ask just how he thought that would be possible without going through proper channels.

It was quite simple he said, "I'll drive to Saigon and commandeer a jet plane and if that fails I will capture a helicopter and force the crew to fly me home."

This was coming from a well-educated man known for his common sense but it was clear his level of stress had overcome his reasoning.

So I sat the man down for a talk. I told him that without a set of orders, he would never be allowed close to a jet plane, it had been tried before. I also explained that we didn't have any helicopters that could fly across the Pacific Ocean without running out of fuel, not to mention how slow it would be. By the way, high jacking a Huey for a quick flight home had been tried unsuccessfully, I might add.

About the only choice a man on the run could make would be trying to cross into Cambodia, or Laos. Either way would cost a great deal of money and probably the fugitives life. Still many men fell into a life of crime without thinking where it might end.

One of the worst reasons I heard in-country came straight from the mouth of a young man being escorted from deep in the Delta to Long Binh, home of the notorious Long Binh Jail. The jail complex was built on top of a hill with the main prison surrounded by a very high chain link fence that was covered with heavy canvas. No one could see out or in. The canvas not only blocked the view but even worse, it blocked any cooling breeze that might happen by. The intense tropical sun bore down on the prison grounds from day light till dark and man-made shade was a scarce item. This young man, a handcuffed prisoner of the Army MP's told how excited he was to be going to Long Binh Jail. He talked on and on about how much better it would be than his normal duty in the Delta. My partner and I were standing near this prisoner and his MP escort and couldn't help overhearing what was being said. The MP's remained quiet throughout this out-pouring of joy but being a dyed in the wool instigator, I had to ask the young prisoner if he had ever seen Long Binh Jail. He smilingly replied no, but it had to be better than where he was at. I told him I didn't know where he had been serving but I knew a little about his destination and that it was bad. I explained the living conditions were bad even by Viet Nam standards and that the men who guarded that facility were hard men and the Commanding Officer was one of the toughest men I had ever met.

The young man gave me a blank look then said, "it couldn't be that bad." He looked to his two MP guards for their thoughts, however their thoughts were directed to me. One of the two MP's that we knew explained they had enough trouble trying to deliver prisoners to LBJ without my stirring up trouble. I knew he was right but I also knew the stories that came out of that canvas covered prison and I felt bad for the young immature soldiers who were led astray by their older but no wiser counterparts. They believed that LBJ was like some work farm or ivy league prison but that is just not true. The Commander and the guards were hard men and they had to be that way. I do not condemn these men for their's was an impossible task and a thankless one at that. I never knew anyone who came out of that facility after their sentence was served nor did I ever hear of anyone making a successful escape.

I had the distinct pleasure of visiting a couple of other military prisons that were considered better than LBJ and they made me a nervous wreck. I knew right off that being in the Army was as close to being incarcerated as I ever wanted to get. I, for one, found staying straight with the Universal Code of Military Justice much easier after just a few minutes behind bars and I was there as a guest.

GARY JAY POOL

TEACHING

The 3rd Herd had the honor of teaching explosive classes to the new MP's. During these instruction classes we displayed many explosive devices both of U.S. manufacture and those of the Viet Cong. A lot of our information was ignored or taken for granted, which was clear by watching the men's faces and overly relaxed manners.

My partner and I felt if we had to stand up and talk for better than an hour in a hot unventilated building, the least the students could do was to stay awake. So we fell back on the use of an old friend, the M-80 fire cracker of which we had an unending supply. If I saw soldiers sleeping or reading, I would catch my partners eye, then he would sneak up behind the culprit and drop a lit M-80 under his seat. It only took a couple of these per class until the group realized it was easier to stay awake.

There were, of course, protests to our training approach. Some of the startled GI's would wake up wanting to fight but that was not a problem because my partner was always up for a scrap. I was told on occasion that one of the unit commanders had called to complain about our tactics and we always offered to relinquish our teaching duties, but the offer was never accepted because no one else wanted the duty.

The real reason we continued the instructions was the hope that maybe one of these new in-country soldiers would pick up a tidbit of information that would prevent their injury or death. The rewarding part came as we learned of instances where what we had imparted did, in fact, save lives.

A few times we even received a thank you from the individuals involved, but we didn't want thanks or awards, all we wanted was to prevent making calls where some GI had been killed or wounded by an explosive device. Death or injury in the name of your country or for a cause is one thing, becoming a statistic because of ignorance is quite another thing.

VIET NAM EOD VETERANS REUNION

For years I had listened to other veterans talk about their military reunions and they would admonish me to be sure to attend mine. I gave the same reply each time, "it will never happen because it's too much work to herd chickens." I explained that remark by saying, "if more than three EOD men were to gather in one place someone would call the law, if five EOD men were to congregate in one place it would constitute a riot, and if ten or more gathered together, the governor would call out the National Guard." There are certain groups of men who adhere more willingly to the laws and customs of society when they operate singly.

However in 2007 several ex-EOD Viet Nam Veterans sent out notices of an upcoming "one time only reunion" to be held in St. Louis, Missouri. Although I couldn't really afford to go for several reasons, I explained to my very understanding wife the miracle of this event. I truly could not foresee it ever happening again. In fact, I doubted as we drove across Missouri that it would ever come to pass this time. But miracle of miracles, about forty EOD attended, many of whom hadn't seen or heard from one another for three and a half decades.

This meeting was for EOD Viet Nam Veterans but as the meeting went by and many of the members wanted to make the reunion a regular event, some clear thinkers explained that we were a small group who would soon pass into history and the organization would cease to exist.

So it was suggested and voted on then and there that we would join the National EOD organization as a sub group. The only provision being that our clerks be admitted as full members. That may sound strange to the rank and file military units but this is one group that is anything but common.

The EOD community is made up of all the U.S. Military branches. We all attended the same school and often times worked together, not just in Viet Nam but around the world. Many of our clerks lived with our units, day and night through the good and bad times. It could be said that these dedicated clerks were the heart and soul of our little units, maybe mother hen or father confessor would be more of a proper description. In any case, it would be difficult for us to imagine being part of an organization without our clerks being involved.

These National EOD reunions have become a yearly affair, I wish now it had become so sooner, allowing us to have known our comrades, wives and children better through the years. Communication between us might have prevented some of the hardships endured during those solitary years. But then I realize most of these men were independent self-sufficient individuals who seldom asked for help. Just part of the make-up of the breed I guess.

Dick Hause & Art Macksey pointing to
the location where the 3rd Ord was stationed at
Long Binh Post

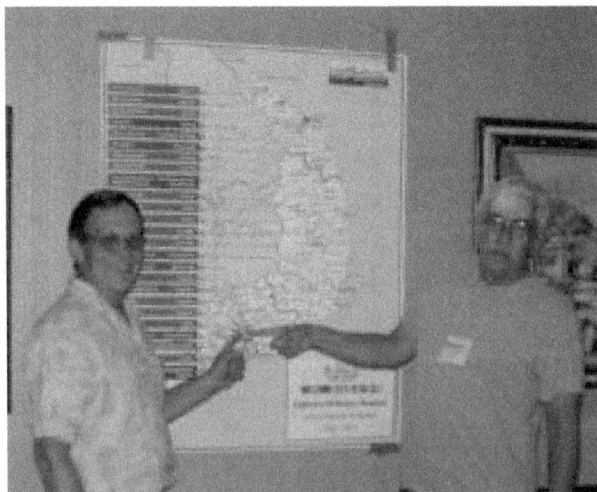

TRIBUTE TO MASTER JACK

This is going to be the most difficult section of this book to write, partially for personnel reasons, also due to the many men who should be named in this last chapter of the 3rd Herd but unfortunately can't be. I don't mean to slight anyone, in most instances I just did not respond to a large enough number of calls with that individual to write interesting tales of these incidents. Some of the omitted members transferred out of or came to the 3rd Herd later in my tour. I hope this to be a tribute to all EOD personnel but, especially, those members of the 3rd Herd who have already passed.

But where to start? Not by rank surely, because those positions meant little to me, still that may be the only fair way to list these men. The first man I must list was our oldest soldier, Jack Summrall or Master Jack as he was best known, not solely for his rank of Master Sergeant in the United States Army. He was truly a master of all he surveyed; he had rules and standards that were to be lived by and woe unto those, be they enlisted or officer, who failed to toe the mark.

I found him to be a fair and honest man, one that possibly worried too much about his men, a rare thing in the Viet Nam War.

Master Jack was a veteran of WWII, Korea, and Viet Nam plus a lot of battles that have never been recorded. I saw a lot of my own father who was a WWII combat veteran, in the words and deeds of Master Jack. These soldiers were a different breed than my generation, for they had met the Devil on his ground and prevailed. These men and women veterans of the Second World War did in fact truly save the world from slavery, tyranny and death.

I have known hundreds of these men and tried my best to interview them, a truly difficult task. I learned that nearly every man I questioned had without admitting so, shown clear signs of the lifelong effects of their ordeal; and yet not one asked for any recompense, not even a thank you. To these veterans fighting and overcoming evil was just what they had to do.

I have, since a young man, made sure that I paid my respect and I hope understanding for any peculiarities they might display.

Master Jack Summrall was a man who received a great deal of respect from those who had any contact with him. It was just a feeling that came over you when in his presence; here was a man who had not only experienced life but also lived it by his code of honor.

Jack Summrall is gone now and I don't expect to see the equal of him again. Truthfully I hope not as those men's metal was truly forged in the heat of battle, life and death struggles not just to win a battle but to save their world.

Master Sgt. Jack Summrall
July 1, 1923.-- November 13, 2015
Jacksonville Memory Gardens,
Orange Park, Florida

GARY JAY POOL

TRIBUTE TO ART MACKSEY

I can remember very well the night the 3rd Ordnance Battalion's Explosive Ordnance Disposal holding area blew up. Stg. Arthur Macksey and I spent the night prowling the depot's pitch black revetments filled with high explosives, responding to urgent calls for help. When our holding or storage area detonated it spewed a wide variety of ordnance across a depot filled with thousands upon thousands of tons of explosive ordnance. The Commanding Officer was ordered to report to the Battalion Commander's office where he passed the night and we were ordered into the depot in hopes of preventing a major disaster. Macksey and I departed immediately and I know that other teams followed but it was so dark after sunset that they could have been standing beside me and I wouldn't have known they were there. I don't recall a lot of radio traffic that night probably because everyone was too busy stumbling around in the dark trying to answer calls from worried depot personnel.

The demands for our services were considered urgent by those needing assistance, some of which became very insistent. Sgt. Macksey remained CALM and unshaken while overbearing officers demanded we respond immediately to their particular hazardous situation. He wisely gave priority to those items that posed the greatest threat to the huge Long Binh ammo depot. It is times like this when the real professional EOD men shine through and Art Macksey was a true bomb disposal expert.

Sgt. Macksey and I spent that long tedious night together scouring the depot for any hazardous situations that we could rectify. The first light of the morning sun revealed just how complete had been the destruction of our holding area by the previous night's explosion, and just how close we had come to destroying the Long Binh Ammunition depot. I counted myself very fortunate to have been teamed with Macksey. We worked together that night and on many other incidents in the Viet Nam War and it was always reassuring to know that Macksey was at my side.

In those days Army EOD traveled in two-man teams without escorts through a hostile country where you learned to survive by your wits while applying any knowledge you may have picked up from the people and their customs. Art Macksey was well versed in the traditions of the Vietnamese people and seemed to know instinctively which tact to take when dealing with these often unpredictable people.

The two-man team theory had both its weakness and strengths in that your partner was the only thing that stood between you and a sad end. He was your only connection to the world if while operating in the field you became ill or injured. A partner had to be loyal and dedicated to his teammate to ensure that both of you returned safely while attempting to complete a mission. A partner must be cool, calm and collected to prevent any mishap while handling explosives or disarming booby traps, but one had to be especially careful in dealing with any human threats which constantly surrounded us. In either case, the tiniest of mistakes could have ended in disaster. Art Macksey was a person whom every team member wanted to partner with, which is saying a lot considering the size of the egos some of us sported in those days. But not Art, he remained quiet and unassuming thru all the hype and bluster.

I always felt confident in Macksey's company and trusted his decisions without question, knowing these delicate decisions had to be infallible and yet made on the spur of the moment without any deliberation. This was an impossible fine line that had to be walked and Macksey was one of the best at negotiating the impossible.

Sgt. Macksey was a man with a quick wit, who always had a kind encouraging word when your spirits were down. He was a person who could find good in every situation and somehow managed without complaint to make the best of the worst that life handed him. Art was a great partner and to use his term, "good people."

I, like many others, are proud and fortunate to have served with Art Macksey. To have teamed with such a man in a theater of war was a blessing for a young inexperienced EOD man like me. Although this is a totally inadequate sentiment, all I can say is "Thank you Sgt. Macksey and May God Bless You."

Arthur William Macksey

August 31, 1940 – July 19, 2008

East Leland Cemetery
Lake Leelanau, Michigan

TRIBUTE TO DICK KORNMANN

I first met Dick Kornmann when he transferred into the 71st Ordnance EOD unit at Wilmington, Ohio, where I was already assigned. He was a fun loving Staff Sergeant with a good sense of humor and an attitude that nothing seemed to bother. When things went wrong he always found the good side of the trouble and made jokes of everything.

I was lucky to work with Dick on a number of calls in the States and learned a lot about the military and how to survive its pitfalls. We received orders for Viet Nam at nearly the same time, in fact, I pulled night duty while the members of the unit gave him and me a going away party. Dick called me several times from the party to relate what a great time everyone was having and how he wished I was there.

Dick arrived in-country shortly before I did and settled in with the 3rd Herd. The day I landed I was standing outside a run-down personnel placement building when he and another 3rd Herder, whom I also knew, came by in a jeep and slid to a halt, they backed up and we talked for a few minutes. When I told them I had orders to go up north, Dick refused to allow it. He jumped out of the jeep and went inside the building, rounded up the clerk who was typing my orders and demanded he change them to read 3rd Ordnance EOD, Long Binh. The clerk argued it was late in the day and all of my paperwork had been done. Still Dick fought on until the clerk changed my duty station to the 3rd Herd.

We loaded up in the jeep and headed for Long Binh where I quickly learned the unit did not want another man. The First Sgt. started yelling at Dick that he didn't want another man, but by that time Dick had disappeared leaving me flat footed with no excuse for being present.

Dick was a good friend, one who would stand beside you as they say through thick and thin. We went on many calls together, laughed a lot, argued a lot, and got into trouble a lot. I'm sure the 3rd Herd NCO's were delighted to have Dick transferred to another unit; they would have been ecstatic if I would have followed suit. In fact, there wasn't a single protest made when Dick and I decided we should go join the Green Beret but there was a lot of grumbling when we returned the same day.

Dick is gone now and I admit to missing the man. He loved to play practical jokes and did his best to get my goat, but after knowing him for a couple of years, I often think back to the many times his good advice kept me on the straight and narrow.

Richard Korman passed away
November 17, 1974.
He is buried at Coal Town Cemetery,
Orvis, MS

TRIBUTE TO SMITTY

When I worked for Master Sgt. Robert Smith or Smitty as we all called him, he was a Sergeant First Class in the United States Army running a ten man EOD unit in Viet Nam. It may sound easy enough, but it was like herding chickens. Every man had his own opinion and seldom were any two alike, we were strong-willed, arrogant men who always thought our way was the best way.

Smitty had the ability to get cooperation from his men without pulling rank or using harsh words. He usually simply asked a person to do something and they quickly fell in line. He never used physical threats as some NCO's, but it was clear he could successfully go that route if need be. He was a jack of all trades, a utility player who was willing to serve in whatever capacity the Army needed.

Smitty was an excellent EOD man, one who really knew his business. He always kept up on the new ordnance and the changing operations in the field. I was twenty five years old the year I spent with Smitty but I truly believe his guidance brought my childish behavior up to par with my true age.

SFC Smith was a man who was often sought out for advice not only from those in ranks below his but also from those many grades above him. His knowledge and acceptance of human response and life itself made him a valuable asset to any undertaking. The man had a set rule about equality for all humans from the lowest to the highest most powerful person, he accepted people as equals no matter their station in life and expected others to do the same.

I think the one unusual trait or gift that Smitty possessed was his ability to make people respond to him in a positive fashion. He seldom gave a direct order but rather persuaded men to do as he suggested without shouting or threating anyone. It was truly inspiring to watch him quietly work his charm on those of a differing opinion, all while wearing a wide smile. Smitty was always on your side and more than willing to back up a point with word or deed. I had several experiences where others would have left me hanging in the wind but, if you were right, Smitty was behind you 100%. I believe Smitty's greatest weakness was concern for his men, as was pointed out to me by some of his superiors.

Smitty had a wife and several children who, I discovered years later while attending his funeral visitation, knew very little about his service career. Obviously he was a man who did not burden his family with worry. I felt truly honored to meet Smitty's family that night and was allowed the time and their polite attention while I recounted many tales of Smitty's service in Viet Nam. They certainly didn't understand EOD, its dangers and the stress that men like Smitty faced in doing their every day jobs. I will tell them now that he led a bomb disposal squad by example, he never wavered in the face of adversity whether it endangered his career or personal safety.

I always enjoyed going on bomb calls with Smitty because he had so much common sense in his approach to people and situations. He was a true EOD senior NCO because if there were chances to be taken, he insisted on being the one to take them.

He was a true patriot, one who put country and service above all else. The man could have easily prospered in the civilian world and been home every night as opposed to his long absences in some faraway place. The large Smith family was a happy lot, the children growing up to be good honorable citizens just as Smitty knew they would.

Smitty was never into material things but

seemed content to help others to attain their goals. He was a religious man who strongly believed in his church and his God but never tried to force his convictions on anyone else.

I praise not only this man but the tens of thousands who have gone before him and the ones who will hopefully follow his lead in protecting this great nation with little regard to their own rise to fame or fortune. How many Smitty's have gone before, never receiving nor wanting recognition? I can't say, but this one will be remembered until those now fading veterans have followed him to his reward.

St. John's Catholic Cemetery
Petersburg, Nebraska

TRIBUTE TO JOHN CLAFFY

The first time I met John Claffy or Big John as he was known, he was a private attending the Naval Ordnance EOD School at Indian Head, Maryland. He was dressed in a suit and was carrying a bible. Big John began to preach to me then insisted that I attend church with him that Wednesday night. My only coat at that time was a well-worn brown leather jacket that had been given to me several years before. It was called an Arizona Bush Jacket; the lining was missing and so were all the pockets, but it did at least zip up. I had it sent to me from home because I didn't have the money to buy a civilian coat, in fact, I was scrapping the bottom of the barrel just to keep up with the expenses required to remain in EOD schooling.

After John saw the brown leather coat and from that decided that I was a Hell's Angel member and I should be avoided at all cost, so we exchanged a few words before he left for church. We had occasion to meet several times while attending EOD school but never in the bar which was located in the basement of our barracks, nor in the bars located in the first three building just outside the main gate which were owned by EOD men who allowed us students to eat and drink on credit.

After leaving Indian Head, my next meeting with Big John was at the 3rd Herd as I met the members of the team residing there. He was now a Spec 4 and a completely different person, or maybe two different people would be more correct. John flipped-flopped from a religious scripter spouting zealot, to a hard drinking two fisted sinner. His demeanor changed by the day and sometimes by the hour, but he was an exceptional EOD man who could be trusted with any situation. He loved people and no matter which personality he was in that day, he always defended the down trodden, being protector of the weak and rejected. John read and wrote letters home for people, always had a shoulder to cry on and I'm sure was an easy touch for those who had money trouble.

Once again I can truthfully say Big John and I worked several interesting bomb calls together, many of these made me glad that he was by my side. I met many men who loved or feared Big John but not a one who refused to go in harm's way with him.

Big John retired at the rank of Major from the U.S. Army, quite a climb for a man with humble beginnings. We spoke on the phone just a few days before his passing. I was thanking him for sending me a beautiful oak barrel top which was engraved with my name, the 3rd Ord and the crab badge. It's a gift I will always cherish from a man I will always think of as my friend.

Two years ago, while on a trip through the southwest, my wife and I made a stop at Big John's grave in the military cemetery at Ft. Bliss, Texas. The area of his stone is grassless sand that is kept clean and raked up. I gave him a hand salute as is proper from an enlisted man to an officer. The military says a hand salute is rendered to the uniform not the man but in this case I was indeed saluting the man, not the uniform.

Thank you Big John.

Big John Claffy

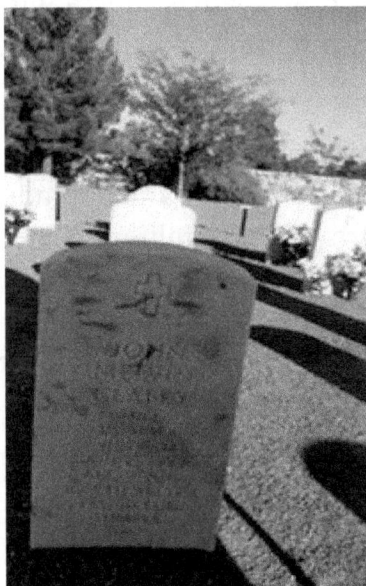

Major John Melvin Claffy
July 5, 1949 – August 9, 2015
Fort Bliss National Cemetery
El Paso, Texas

TRIBUTE TO JIM POINDEXTER

Staff Sgt. James Poindexter, U.S. Air Force was a big man with a heart to equal his immense size. He was a southern boy from Lawton, Oklahoma with a drawl and a never-ending bag of humorous stories and poignant tales of life. Jim truly had the gift of gab but he also had a great deal of tact and a sense of when to approach a sensitive subject and when to wait for a better time.

Jim and I met at Anniston Army Depot upon beginning the Chemical School, the beginning phase of EOD schooling. I would never have been able to complete EOD School if not for Jim's help, guidance, and understanding. He took me under his wing, explaining the facts of military life and aiding me in obtaining my goal to be an EOD man.

I don't believe I ever really said thank you to Jim for all of his kindness to a poor uneducated boy from the Iowa's Missouri River bottoms. I sincerely thank you, Jim Poindexter for being a friend and helping me to be a better person. Thank You.

In Remembrance

James Frederick Poindexter
"Jimmy"
February 23, 1943
August 5, 2011

James Poinkexter

Union Presbyterian Church Cemetery
South Carolina

A SPECIAL THANK YOU

I assume many people will read these tributes to those who have passed and begrudge my taking up space to thank them for sharing my life. I could do a whole book about the people living and dead who have affected my life for the good. However, I singled out these men who are no longer living because they gave me the gift of themselves.

The same is true of so many men still living that I have not seen or had contact with over the last nearly fifty years, all of these, the living and the departed, live on in my mind every day and somehow I feel they are still part of this world.

I tried to tell the story of EOD through the lives of the men I knew in my first book, Xuc May. I now realize, after talking for ten years to people who read those stories that I failed miserably to show the heart and soul of these loyal patriotic men. I doubt if this attempt will be any more successful than the last but I want to extend a sincere thank you to all the men and women, whoever they may be, who have over the last two hundred and fifty years donned the various uniforms of our country. To you, a well-deserved heart felt THANK YOU FOR YOUR SERVICE.

AN EOD MAN

1. **AS SEEN BY THE DEPARTMENT OF DEFENSE:**
An overpaid, over ranked tax burden that is indispensable because he has volunteered to go anywhere, do anything, anytime, as long as he can booze it up, brawl, steal jeeps, corrupt women, lie, wear a Star Sapphire ring, a Seiko watch and a demo knife.

2. **AS SEEN BY HIS COMMANDER:**
A fine specimen of a drinking, jeep stealing, brawling, woman corrupting liar, with a Star Sapphire ring, a Seiko watch and a demo knife.

3. **AS SEEN BY HIS WIFE:**
A stinking member of the family who comes home once a year with a rucksack full of dirty clothes, stale booze on his breath and a bunch of war stories.

4. **AS SEEN BY HIMSELF:**
A tall, highly trained, handsome professional killer, female idol, Star Sapphire ring wearing, demo knife carrying gentleman, who is always on time thanks to the reliability of his Seiko watch and his stolen jeep.

5. **AS SEEN BY OTHER EOD MEN:**
A drunken brawling, jeep stealing, woman corrupting liar, wearing a Star Sapphire ring, a Seiko watch and a demo knife.

ABOUT THE AUTHOR

Gary Jay Pool was born July 18, 1946 to a poor southwest Iowa farm family.

His family consisted of his father who was a World War II veteran and a man of few words; his mother who was an insatiable reader and avid conversationalist; and an older sister.

Being raised on a dead-end dirt road very near the Missouri River, Gary spent countless hours hunting and fishing and became an avid outdoorsman. The author's father spent his life trying to raise his only son to survive being a soldier in a war, he somehow knew was coming. This training fell in line with Gary's choice to serve in the United States Army. A tour of duty in Vietnam in Army Bomb Disposal provided the wealth of factual antidotes for his first book, Xuc May.

Having a lifelong passion for writing, Gary has written several other stories which he plans to finalize and publish during his retirement years. Today Gary and his wife Jan live in Tabor, Iowa where they raised four daughters. His wife and daughters all work as a team to help publish and sell his books.

Watch for the latest updates and new books on Gary's website www garyjaypool.com or follow his Facebook page www.facebook.com/garyjaypoolpublishing.com

OTHER BOOKS BY GARY JAY POOL

XUC MAY (Never Happen) – Non-fiction

The Captain & The Candles – Fiction

Shanks Crossing – Fiction

* 9 7 8 1 7 3 2 1 5 7 4 2 2 *